OUR STRUGGLE: EAST ASIA CALLING

V N Krishna Pillai

Notion Press

Old No. 38, New No. 6
McNichols Road, Chetpet
Chennai - 600 031

First Published by Notion Press 2019
Copyright © V N Krishna Pillai 2019
All Rights Reserved.

ISBN 978-1-64546-494-5

Dedication

This book is dedicated to the memory of the great Indian revolutionary Rash Behari Bose, the father of the Indian independence movement in East Asia and those countless brave sons and daughters of India who sacrificed their lives in the battle for freedom.

VNK Pillai

Contents

About the Author

Vathukottu Narayana Pillai Krishna Pillai (VNK) was born in Chengannur, Kerala, on 7 August 1911, as the eighth son of his parents Devaki Amma and Narayana Pillai. VNK's father was a well-to-do farmer and a man of good repute in Chengannur. After high school education in Chengannur, he joined H.H. The Maharaja's College of Science, Trivandrum and continued his studies till he completed BA degree in 1934.

Early in 1936, VNK started work as an insurance agent for The Empire of India Life Assurance Company, Bombay (now Mumbai), and became the Travancore state representative of the company by the end of the year. However, the company had to cease operations in Travancore from September 1937 due to the hostile action taken by the then (notorious) Diwan of Travancore, Sir C.P. Ramaswami Iyer.

Unable to find a job, VNK decided to go to Malaya (Malaysia). He sailed out in November 1939, when World War II was raging in Europe. He was married just four days before he sailed to Penang. He failed to get a job in Malaya but secured a teacher's post in a Chinese school in Kuching, Sarawak, Borneo. It was a well-paid job and put him at ease.

The Japanese occupation of Borneo in December 1940 suddenly threw him out of job. During March 1941, he organised the Indian Independence League of Borneo and was the secretary-general of the organisation there. VNK also edited and published the Azad Hind weekly from Borneo. At the end of May 1941, he went to Bangkok as the leader of a five-man delegation from Borneo to the Indian Independence Conference held there during June-July 1941.

And when the Indian Independence League headquarters was established in Bangkok, he was appointed a secretary of the secretariat there. There he was associated with S.A. Iyer, N. Shivram, B.K. Das, A.M. Sahay and A.M. Nair. Rash Behari Bose was the president and head of the organisation.

Broadcasting over the Azad Hind Radio, Bangkok interested him much and his news commentaries in Malayalam were well received. When things went wrong in Malaya and Gen Mohan Singh disbanded the INA in Singapore, Rash Behari Bose decided to shift the League headquarters to Singapore and the stupendous task of shifting the entire stores was entrusted to VNK. He had to travel from Bangkok to Singapore – a distance of about 400 km – in a goods train, a dangerous journey at that time.

In Singapore, he attended the conference of Indian representatives held before and after the arrival of Netaji there. When Netaji reorganised the IIL headquarters, VNK was appointed head of the overseas department. Netaji lauded the excellent work done by VNK.

After the surrender of the INA in August 1945, the British military authorities ill-treated and detained him for more than 13 months. Thereafter, he was not allowed to go back to Borneo or to return home. Even in those hard days VNK did his best to help the Indians in Borneo, who were very harshly and cruelly treated by the occupation forces. And, for this, he made representations to the panel of lawyers.

Pandit Kunzru, the then Congress president Jawaharlal Nehru and other political leaders visited Malaya at that time. VNK also sought the help of Mr. Chettur, the then Agent-General of India in Singapore. Finally, he succeeded in getting Barrister K.P. Keshava Menon to represent Indians who were unjustly treated and persecuted by the British in Borneo. In this regard, Mr. Sapru did his best to influence the Indian government.

After 13 months in Singapore, VNK managed to get a permit to leave for India. This was managed with help of friends in Kuala Lumpur.

This book was written during VNK's enforced stay in Singapore and was rewritten after Independence. Many books have been published giving accounts of the INA and the war of freedom it fought but there has never been published a book giving an authentic and comprehensive history of the movement and the struggle. The news of the last moments of Netaji is still fresh in the minds of the Indian people.

Back home, VNK again failed to secure a job with the Government of India though many of his old compatriots landed decent jobs. He got some monetary help from the home ministry and a small pension from the government of Kerala. He was awarded with a Tamraptra in 1974 and a pension from the central government later.

Preface

In this book I have made an earnest and sincere effort to present to the reader a brief and authentic account of the Indian independence movement in Southeast Asia, which started side by side with the 'Greater East Asia War' of Japan. The Japanese gave the Indians a chance to organise an army and liberate India from the British. Two great leaders, Rash Behari Bose and Netaji Subhash Chandra Bose, organised and directed this war against the Anglo-Saxon forces for a period of eighteen months. In spite of the spectacular victories in the early stages, the INA suffered defeat in the end. But it is an indisputable fact that the war of liberation waged by the INA contributed a great deal to the attainment of India's independence.

After bitter and strenuous struggle for more than a century and after sacrificing millions of India's worthy sons and daughters, India achieved freedom. But our struggle is not yet over. Noble and mighty efforts and great sacrifices India made in securing the freedom of Bangladesh is surely a part of our struggle.

The father of our nation Mahatma Gandhi said: "Strive on until oppression has been banished from India; strive on until in every nation and in every climate in the East and the West, in the North and the South, freedom for man and woman shall possess the earth. Then, and not until then can humanity allow the flag to be unfurled; strive on."

I was an active member of the Indian independence movement in Southeast Asia from its very beginning and held responsible positions in the organisation. I organised the Indian Independence League of Borneo and was its general secretary. I had taken part in all the Indian and joint Indo-Japanese conferences held in Bangkok and Singapore. I was the general secretary of the Indian Independence League headquarters in Bangkok when I carried out the shifting of the headquarters from Bangkok to Singapore, at the end of March 1943. And, when Netaji reorganised the Indian Independence League headquarters, I had worked closely with most of the civil and military leaders of the movement.

Rash Behari Bose, like an affectionate uncle, was very kind and considerate to me. I have had the opportunity to interact with Netaji on various occasions on official matters and report to him on the affairs of the 212-odd branches of the Indian Independence League in East Asia. I used to hold personal talks with Netaji on important matters of the movement. He liked my work and highly commended me.

I was a member of the various committees appointed by Netaji. I was one of the few civilian officers who attended the last meeting addressed by him in Singapore on 15 August 1945, before his departure to Japan the next morning that was also perhaps his final journey.

The manuscript of this book was prepared during my enforced rest in Singapore, in the later part of 1945. I received useful information and help from the INA officers and members of the Indian Independence League in Southeast Asia, particularly in Rangoon and Bangkok as also from a few Japanese and other foreign friends.

Comrades of 329 Bukit Timah Road, Singapore were very affectionate to me and their help was of great importance in preparing this manuscript. I express my sincere thanks to one and all of them.

This book is divided into two parts, each devoted to depicting successive events and developments under Rash Behari Bose and Netaji Subhash Chandra Bose. Whenever any reference is made to the situation or state of affairs of the Indian people in Southeast Asia, it is done on the most trustworthy and reliable information that could be obtained. References to persons are made only when necessary and are made after careful study and with a great deal of fairness.

I have attempted to sketch the background, for which I may not be fully competent to comment. However, I have stated briefly what I have learnt. Giving a title for the book has been a difficult problem for me. The original title 'Our Movement' was later changed to 'Our Struggle,' which, I later felt, was more appropriate. Finally, I felt a change of tone was needed to describe earlier events and hence the new title 'Our Struggle: East Asia Calling.'

I have given full texts of the resolutions passed at early conferences and some of the speeches and statements of Rash Behari Bose and other leaders. These are useful for the proper understanding of the movement in general. I have omitted some of the speeches of Netaji in the second part of the book as they have been published elsewhere.

It is now nearly three quarters of a century since I first planned this book. It was abridged twice and necessary alterations made to suit the changes brought about by the attainment of freedom.

The long delay in publishing this book is mainly due to my inability to get the right publisher. Also, it was my pious hope and great desire to find out the truth of Netaji's whereabouts and to complete this book along with authentic news of our great leader.

I was told the last moments of Netaji were most unexpected and very cruel – that like the Mahatma, Netaji too was shot dead and that the Godse in this case was an unknown Japanese. I have given details on how I learned about this in the last pages under the title – Epilogue. I could not verify the facts yet.

I do not think that the delay in publishing this book will ever diminish its usefulness or credibility. So far, no such book has been published and none will ever be published. I am very happy that this book is published on the 75th anniversary of the establishment of the Indian Independence League and the Indian national Army.

JAI HIND

VNK Pillai

The Background

Aryans invaded India between 3000 and 1500 BC; they made themselves the dominant people and embraced the Hindu religion, which was the religion of the people of Hindustan. In AD 788, the Mohammedan conquests began and in the 15th century India came under their suzerainty. But, in the 18th century, the Empire having begun to decay was divided into provinces, which were virtually independent states.

Meanwhile, Portuguese, French and English merchants founded outposts on the coasts of India and their companies became very powerful. They began to take sides in internal wars of Indian princesses even as they fought among themselves for power. The war between the alien powers ended in 1763 by the entire elimination of French influence in India.

The British made other conquests with their masterly cunningness and treachery and, towards the end of the 18th century the British, as represented by the powerful East India Company, controlled all parts of Hindustan. Servants of this company introduced a cold and steady form of exploitation that drained the lifeblood of the land. Clive, who came as an indignant youth, made a huge fortune by successfully engineering palace revolutions.

Ever since, the Indian people were subjected to an alien rule of oppression, suppression, murder, loot and organised exploitation unknown in history. India yearned for freedom but her strong and cunning enemy forced her to crawl on with the chains of slavery.

After their first defeat at the hands of the British in the year 1757 in Bengal, the Indian people fought a series of hard and bitter wars over a stretch of 100 years. The history of this period is full of examples of unparalleled heroism and self-sacrifices of countless Indian patriots. Unfortunately, for India, her sons at first did not at all realise that the British constituted a grave threat to the country and they did not, therefore, put up a united fight against the enemy.

Ultimately, when the Indian people were roused to the reality of the situation, they made a concerted move and under the flag of Bahadur Shah, in 1857, fought their last war as free people. In spite of a series of brilliant victories in the early stages of the war, ill-luck and faulty leadership gradually brought about their final collapse and subjugation. In that tragic year, the crown of England took control of the East India Company. The British government also appointed a secretary of state for India in London. And, in 1858, Queen Victoria proclaimed herself as the Empress of India; Viscount Canning was appointed the first Viceroy and Governor-General of India.

India was a rich country before the destiny of its unfortunate people fell into the hands of the British. A highly organised trade in India sent its textiles, lace, weapons, muslins, Kashmiri shawls, superior wool and spices all over the world. Since India, however, had no need for European wears, precious metals acted as payments for costly exports. Gold and silver thus flowed from the West to the East. Thus India became the treasure chamber of the world.

India was not only fabulously rich but also culturally and spiritually the leading nation for thousands of years. The moral standards of the present day civilized nations of the world are admittedly a gift of India. Historians record that India had a navy and an army of her own some 6000 years before the West ever had elementary knowledge of the art of warfare.

With the wealth plundered from India, the British revolutionised their industry and expanded trade. And, in order to carry on this trade, the British navy was made more and more powerful so that it could once boast of possessing the most powerful navy in the world. The more powerful the British became, the more they plundered India and the more harshly they treated the people of India.

They forced Indians, whom they trained in their army, to fight in other parts of the world, to conquer more lands, to enslave more people and to make the British Empire mightier. The British Empire thus created and established comprised a fourth of the globe and Britons reigned supreme so that the sun never set in the empire.

It is true that Britain officially abolished slave trade in the empire in the year 1834, but the Indians, apart from being sweated labourers in factories, mines and malaria-infested plantations, suffered under another system no less harsh than the old slave system. The slave-like treatment of the Indian workers, men, women and children well matched the plunder of the land, the destruction of handicrafts and the exploitation of the poor peasants of Hindustan. Thus, when one knows by what methods Britain achieved her aims and how the people, "happy under British rule," had not only to sacrifice their freedom but were forced to part with their natural means of existence, cheated of the fruits of their hard labour and pressed into a system of slavery, will surely turn in sordid history. The British by their deceit and lies bluffed the whole world for well nigh two centuries about the black man's burden.

What did it matter to the British, if Indian children at an age when in other places they would happily be at play, were forced to work in factories, inhaling smoke and dust, leading to ill-health and early death? The main concern of the white sahibs in India was to ever increase sources from which revenues could be raised – by obtaining raw materials cheap and establishing a good market for their machine-made products.

Forcibly disarmed by the British after 1857 and subjected to terror and brutality unparalleled in human history, the Indian people lay prostrate for a while. But, with the birth of the Indian National Congress in 1885 till the end of the First World War, the Indian people, in their endeavour to recover their lost liberty, tried all possible and peaceful methods and co-operated with the satanic British. But, this co-operation with the devil was of no useful purpose. Ultimately, in 1920, when the Indian people, haunted by a new sense of failure, were groping in the dark for a new method, Mahathma Gandhi came forward with the new weapons of non-violence, non-co-operation and civil disobedience, to force the British to obey the will of the Indian people.

For two decades thereafter the Indian people went through a phase of intense patriotic activity on a nation-wide scale. The message of freedom was carried to every Indian home. Through personal example, people were taught to suffer, to sacrifice and to die for the cause of freedom. From the centre to the remotest villages people got knit together into one political organisation – the Indian National Congress. Thus the Indian people not only recovered their political consciousness, but also became a political entity once again.

On the first day of the year 1930, after the Congress' one-year ultimatum for dominion status expired, the Congress made complete independence its new creed, at the Lahore session. And, after the failure of the 1930 movement, the Congress passed the resolution on the fundamental rights, incorporating all the basic demands of the toiling masses.

After the failure of the second Round Table Conference and the second Civil Disobedience Movement of 1932–34 led by Jawaharlal Nehru, the Congress took a different path and reoriented its policy in a manner to build it up as the united national front of the Indian people. Under his leadership, the Congress, the trade unions and kisan workers began to organise and the Congress membership reached records, which made earlier numbers look really small. Thus, the national movement as a whole became stronger and the Indian National Congress grew to its greatness by uniting the ranks of the various patriotic elements in the country and serving the people.

The long history of the Indian National Congress, the great services and the tremendous sacrifices of its many leaders, organisers and workers, the sufferings, the humiliations, torture and murder to which men, women and children of India were subjected to by the British tyrants and their hirelings, are all recorded by worthy men of eminence. There is hardly a day in the century-long British rule in India without an act committed against innocent Indians for the mere crime of loving their country and serving its rightful cause.

Great Indian leaders – loved and respected not only by Indians but by all civilised people the world over, men who were worthy of the highest position in any great country, men like Mahatma Gandhi, Jawaharlal Nehru, Abdul Kalam Azad, Subhash Chandra Bose and Rajagopalachari and others – have all been persecuted and jailed by the British Raj in India.

There is hardly an Indian patriot who was not ill-treated by the British. There were times when the British held in their prisons more than 300,000 men and women for the mere crime of patriotism. Major parts of the lives of great leaders of India were spent in the dark cells of the British prison. The world has no parallel for this.

Forces that are known to threaten the very existence of life, namely, hunger, poverty, disease and famine, are the very forces that give birth to revolutions. These forces, destructive as they are, provide an ideal germinating ground for the seeds of revolution. Revolutions have always been the great expedience of history, which aim at the liberation of nations from tyrannical rule. The revolution, which started in India on 8 August 1942, was, therefore, the outcome of these forces, which have been sapping the nation's vitality. The cause of the cultural and social anaemia of India was the parasite called 'British

Imperialism.' The gigantic August revolution shook the whole of India and it very nearly paralysed the British authority for some time.

Let me now draw your attention to the conditions of Indians abroad, especially in Southeast Asia.

The British exploitation of India forced millions of Indians to go abroad in search of better living conditions. Of these there were more than two million in Southeast Asia. They were in Japan, China, Indo-China, Thailand, Burma, Malaya, the Indies and all over the Pacific islands. The bulk of them, however, were in Malaya and Burma – all human beings with a past and with passions, temptations, errors, thoughts and questions as other subject people elsewhere.

More than eighty per cent of the Indians in Burma and Malaya were labourers; some were skilled, while the majority of them were unskilled. Labelled as British subjects – that cursed mark of slavery – the Indians in these and other parts of Southeast Asia were subjected to the strict control of 'His Imperial Britannic Majesty's rule.' They had full freedom to obey the white sahibs. Kept in ignorance and poverty, these Indians suffered their day-to-day existence.

The lot of the Indian coolly was a strange and peculiar one. His was a life without standards. Kept in memories which were fading, and a health wreaked long ago, he had to toil all day to fill his hungry stomach.

Malaya is now a very rich country. Had it not been for the hundreds of thousands of labourers from India and their hard toil, Malaya would never have been what it is today. Deep under the shadows of the healthy rubber trees, the tall coconut trees and the stout oil palms lie bleached bones of the poor Indian labourers. What is true of Malaya is true of Burma or Borneo and wherever there were Indian labourers.

In Burma, Malaya, Thailand and Japan, there were a few Indians who, by virtue of their patriotism, spread the message of India's freedom. Political exiles like Rash Behari Bose and Raja Mahendra Pratab in Japan, Baba Asman Khan in Java and Baba Amar Singh in Bangkok were prominent patriots.

There were many Indian associations in Burma, Malaya and at other places where there were Indians. And some of them existed for a long time. The Central Indian Association of Malaya was an organised institution. There was an Indian Independence League in Tokyo, Japan and an Indian National Association in Shanghai, China. The activities of all these organisations were mostly symbolic.

There is an old saying that Malaya is the political backwaters of India and another, which says that the "Indians in Thailand should be drowned in the Bay of Bengal."

But, in the hour of trial and suffering, these Indians stood united as never before and did what their leaders told them to do; they did these in the hope of serving their motherland. Their attempt apparently failed but their services remain and are now recognised by the mother country.

In spite of the 16-odd vile attempts by the British to crush the urge of the Indian people, Britain failed, and the surrender of that over-proud and haughty imperialist to the freedom fighters of Hindustan had become a historical fact. India is free now. It is also certain that if there ever remained any shadow of that imperialism anywhere in the world these would long have been wiped out by the progressive forces of the world today. Gone are the days of Fascism and Imperialism and the empires which fostered them.

PART I
Rash Behari Bose Leads Indians in Southeast Asia

"There was silence and then oblivion,

And, from somewhere beyond the void,

The voice of the Holy One spoke once more;

"My duty is done, you complete the task,

The path is clear; March on India,

March on victory."

And those who heard the voice marched and sung 'The song of India's liberty.'

The Indian independence movement in Southeast Asia came into being along with the "Greater East Asia War of Japan." In certain respects it was a stupendous Indian effort, while in certain aspects it was inspired by the Japanese and the circumstances created by the victories of the Japanese armed forces.

On 8 December 1942, the day Japan started the war, a group of Indians assembled at a meeting in Tokyo formed a committee with Rash Behari Bose as the president. Two hours after this, at about 6.00 p.m., another meeting of the Indians in Tokyo was held at the Rainbow Grill. There was an informal discussion to decide the future activities of the committee. It was decided to send representatives to Shanghai to organise the Indian independence movement there. Raja Mahendra Pratap, the well-known Indian revolutionary in Japan, was safely kept out of the picture.

It should be remembered that Raja Mahendra Pratap was the founder, organiser as well as the premier of the Provisional Government of Free India, formed outside India during the First World War. He then had his headquarters in Afghanistan. The reason for the absence of such a leader on the committee or meetings of Indians in Japan was proof enough that the Japanese had no confidence or trust left in the old man. He was not only barred from mixing with the other Indians but was kept a prisoner in the suburb of Tokyo.

The war progressed in favour of the Japanese. They won everywhere. The much-boasted British army ran the length of a thousand miles down Thailand and Malaya before surrendering. A force of a hundred thousand men, comprising Indians, Australians and English surrendered unconditionally to the Japanese General Yamashita, at Singapore, on the 15th of February 1942. The fall of this mighty fortress of the British Empire in the East thrilled the world. It was a pleasant surprise to Indians everywhere.

Whatever might be the cause of this great victory of the Japanese forces over the British, there was no doubt that the help and assistance given to them by the Indians, civil and military, were of great value to them. The Japanese army commanders in the various theaters of

Southeast Asia, their high command as well as the Imperial Majesty paid glowing tributes to services of these men and acknowledged it publicly.

As was the custom of the British, they put the Indian soldiers in the forefront of the battle. They did it in Malaya, Burma, Borneo and Hong Kong. Ill-equipped for a modern war and without air support, some of them fought bravely and died in the field of honour. Many surrendered to the enemy and others joined the Japanese side. Many an Indian civilian helped the Japanese soldiers fight the British. Many crossed the firing lines risking their lives to contact the Indian soldiers and to persuade them not to fight for the British. Their propaganda had good results and they were able to win the confidence of many soldiers.

Sardar Pritam Singh was the leader of the Indian civilians who engaged in such work of sabotaging the loyalty of Indian soldiers to the British.

Captains Mohan Singh and Akram Khan of the British Indian Army posted in northern Malaya were the two outstanding officers who joined the Japanese side. They joined within two weeks of the Japanese attack on Malaya. They rendered great service to the Japanese; they gave valuable information and took an active part in defeating the British. A few hundred Indian soldiers under their command came in the forefront of the Japanese army. They helped the Japanese make an easy crossing from Johore to Singapore. At the time of surrender, Mohan Singh had some 10,000 men on his side.

It is not correct to say that all those who joined the Japanese side did so out of patriotism. But it is also true that at the bottom of their hearts there was hatred towards the British and the very thought of accelerating the destruction of at least a part of their haughty empire might have been a source of joy to all those soldiers.

The assurance of the Japanese that they would help in the formation of an Indian National Army was looked upon as a great favour-to-be by the Indians in Southeast Asia in general and Captain Mohan Singh and his men in particular.

The Japanese did not treat the Indians as enemy nationals, even though they were British subjects and did not loot, plunder or murder Indian soldiers who surrendered to them or were captured in different places. And, in all cases, they were treated better than the white soldiers.

But, in Hong Kong, Borneo and in the jungles of Malaya, the Japanese soldiers tortured to death many Indian prisoners of war. The Indian soldiers who were taken care of and well treated were under the impression that the Japanese were very kind to all Indians.

Saradar Pritam Singh was a highly placed Japanese agent. He organised and founded the Independence League of India with its head office in Bangkok, Thailand and established branches in about thirteen centers in Malaya. Prominent Indians of the localities were appointed presidents. N. Raghavan of Penang, who was the president of the Central Indian Association of Malaya, was the president of the League in Penang. The membership of these League branches was not very small.

On 24 December 1941, an organisation called the Indian National Council of Thailand took shape in

Bangkok, mainly by the efforts of Swami Satyananda Puri, an Indian scholar of good repute in that country. This organisation was recognised by the Thai government and was supported by the Japanese who occupied and controlled Thailand.

Field Marshal Pibun Songram, the premier of Thailand, in a message to the Indian National Council said among other things: "Now all the Asians have risen in one mind to fight against this injustice of the past (Anglo-Saxon exploitation of Asia) and recover and perpetuate the honour and freedom of Asia. This is the greatest mission of our life. Thailand has co-operated with Japan to visualise this great mission. I am, therefore, happy to find that the Indians have also joined us. We shall be comrades in life and comrades in death, so that Asia may be for the Asians."

The Indian National Council collected money for propaganda, organising volunteers and for a regular radio programme over the Bangkok Radio. Swami Satyananda Puri broadcast a message to India on 30 December 1941 over this radio. After giving an analysis of the situation in East Asia, where the tide of war was in favour of Japan, with particular stress on Thailand and the Indians there, he gave a call to revolt against the British authorities, to wipe out the stigma of slavery.

The Indians in East Asia closely followed the developments in Tokyo, Bangkok and elsewhere in East Asia. They strained their ears to listen to the Axis radio stations. They yearned to learn about the reactions to such developments in their homes in India. There was hardly a chance. The anti-India radio in New Delhi did not even spare a chance broadcast to indicate things of this sort.

Indians in Tokyo, Thailand, Shanghai, Borneo, Hong Kong and such other places, from where the Anglo-Saxon powers and their influence were eliminated, gathered together to form organisations for a united fight for India's freedom. The appeals of Netaji Subhash Chandra Bose, Rash Behari Bose and assurances of help from Japanese premier Tojo gave the Indians some encouragement.

When the Japanese attacked the British in Malaya, the majority of Indians, numbering about seven lakh, were not clear in their minds as to their reactions. There were the usual and futile efforts by the British to evacuate the Indians, resulting in considerable panic in public minds.

The British rule in Malaya of the immediate past was a bitter experience to the majority of Indians there. The shooting of the estate labourers who struck work demanding an increase in wages in keeping with the rising costs of living and subsequent prejudicial acts like ordering censorship of Indian-owned newspapers and other similar acts produced a spirit of repressed antagonism in the Indian minds towards them. Again, the strife over the use of the Singapore swimming pool by the Indian army officers caused disaffection to the British.

And, when the Japanese forced the British to surrender Malaya, Indians were ready to welcome the Japanese, not so much out of love for them or trust in their sincerity as by a sense of satisfaction over the defeat of the British.

Two days after the fall of Singapore, on 17 February 1942, Major Fuggier of the Japanese military headquarters in Singapore invited a few Indians, including two prominent barristers. The Major said Japan was prepared to give all assistance to Indians in organising themselves to fight for the liberation of India. He further said that Japan was not treating Indians as enemy nationals. He suggested the organisation of an Indian Independence League to fight for the freedom of India. The Indians listened with interest and took leave after assuring to call on him after consulting Indian patriots, particularly N. Raghavan of Penang.

Meanwhile, Rash Behari Bose invited Indian representatives from Malaya for a conference in Tokyo. Indians gathered in Singapore and the leaders met on 9 and 10 March 1942. The meeting of Indians, in which some Indians from Thailand also participated, decided to send a goodwill mission to Tokyo. The Japanese, however, preferred an official delegation.

The Tokyo Conference

The Indian Independence Conference in Tokyo was held under the chairmanship of Rash Behari Bose, at Sanno Hotel, Tokyo, Japan, from Saturday, 20 March to Monday, 30 March 1942. The goodwill mission from Malaya to the conference included N. Raghavan, K.P. Keshava Menon, S.C. Goho, Col Naranjan Singh Gill and Captain Mohan Singh. Others who attended the meeting were representatives from Hong Kong, Shanghai and Japan.

A 1942 image of Tokyo Railway Station

A plane carrying four delegates to the conference crashed on Mount Fuji near the Issae Bay of Japan. All the occupants, including the Japanese, perished. Swami Satyananda Puri, the leader of the delegation, was a good scholar of repute in Thailand and a friend of the Thai government. He was the chairman of the Indian Independence League of Thailand. The three other members of the delegation were Captain Akram Khan, the brave Indian soldier and intimate of Captain Mohan Singh, Sardar Pritam Singh, an Indian revolutionary who did his best to persuade Indian soldiers not to fight against the Japanese, and K.A. Neelakanda Iyer who was a popular insurance man from Malaya.

The relevant portions from the proceedings of the conference are stated below as officially recorded:

"Rash Behari Bose opened the conference at 2.00 p.m. with a welcome address to the delegates and other gentlemen present and requested their whole-hearted co-operation in the attainment of the common objective, viz, complete independence of India. At the outset, the chairman expressed his heart-felt condolence on the sad demise of the four colleagues who were to attend the conference, stood up and offered profound respect to the departed souls. The conference resolved to send letters of condolence to the bereaved families, and N. Raghavan undertook this responsibility.

Col Iwakuro, who attended the conference representing the government of Japan, gave a welcome address to the members on behalf of the government of Japan. He expressed his whole-hearted support to the conference in its honourable efforts to achieve independence of India. He read out the message of Premier Hidaki Tojo of Japan:

"It is a great pleasure to greet you at this conference, which would make the birth of a new India. Today, your dual ideal of 'Independence of India' and 'India for Indians' over

which you have been most concerned, is going to be realised before long, because it is my belief that the outbreak of this war has created an opportunity which is most favourable for its realisation. If you lose this golden opportunity by being cowardly, lazy or too much involved in mutual antagonism, you and your dependants will remain as slaves for nobody knows how long. The objective world situation is rapidly changing. It is your mission to prepare fully and immediately so as to adjust yourselves to the fact of changing times and to liberate India from the British yoke. We, the Japanese, are prepared to give spiritual and material aid to your revolutionary task, without any compensation or condition. It is needless to say that our common enemy, Britain, will employ every means, such as deceit, bribery, 'divide and rule policy' and threats. On these points we must be very cautious.

"Heaven helps those who help themselves... Indian independence cannot be a gift from anybody, far less from India's enemy, England, from whom you can only expect oppression. India's able leaders must make good use of the surrounding international conditions in order to lessen the amount of sacrifices involved. On her part, what Japan expects from India is that she should do away with all the retarding ideas of religious and class antagonism and the various rivalries between political and military ways of thought and become a united body of 400,000,000 to proceed along the path of independence, that she should realise that the realisation of India's independence in itself is a great revolution that can be led to success only on the strength of her leaders' firm determination, and of the fiery patriotism of all the Indians, and that realising that action is superior to hundreds of arguments. She should make use of the conditions surrounding her to advance the attainment of independence.

And we wish to assure that Japan has not the slightest territorial or political ambition on India and that she will not hesitate to extend any help to the Indians in their fight without any ulterior motive.

Please take your own time and engage yourselves in calm deliberations so that you may arrive at a plan of action which may be beneficial on all parts for the future of India as well as the future of East Asia. This is my request to you all and it comes from the bottom of my heart."

N. Raghavan on behalf of the conference thanked Col Iwakuro and through him the Japanese premier, the government and the people of Japan for their kind encouragement, assistance and worthy promises.

The conference then took up the Indians' attitude towards the war and read out the following resolution which was then passed unanimously.

"Whereas we believe that this war of Greater East Asia is sure to destroy British influence and power in Asia; and whereas we believe that this is a golden opportunity for the realisation of India's national goal, which is nothing but complete independence; and whereas depending upon the self-conscious efforts of various Asiatic nations, a new Asia is sure to arise as a result of this war; we hereby resolve that we must join hands with Japan, in accordance with the declared policy of the Imperial Japanese government, made through Premier Tojo on the occasion of the fall of Singapore."

After further discussions, in which all members participated, it was resolved that 'Unity,' 'Faith' and 'Sacrifice' shall be the guiding principles of the independence movement.

The conference fully clarified the meaning of complete independence for India and passed the following resolution unanimously:

"That independence complete and free from foreign domination, interference or control of whatever nature shall be the object of the movement and, in the opinion of the conference, now is the right time to achieve the object and secure such independence."

In order to spread the independence movement in East Asia, it was decided that all possible steps such as broadcasts, newspaper articles, pamphlets, lectures and demonstrations be made to serve the purpose. It was also decided that contacts with the Indian National Congress and Indian leaders be established.

The meeting also unanimously made the following decisions regarding the organisation:

1. Local branches of leagues are to be formed for the duration of the war whose presidents are to be elected by the committee formed at a meeting of the representatives of the place. Vacancies on the committee are to be filled by majority vote by the committee members. The presidents are not removable without the vote of three-fourths of the members of the committee.

2. The presidents of the various local bodies together with the representatives of the Indian Army in East Asia, which shall not exceed the total number of civilian members of the committee, will form the committee of representatives, which will lay down the general policy of action and elect a Council

of Action consisting of a president and four staff members of whom two shall be from the military.

3. The Council of Action shall be responsible for working out the general policy and they shall appoint departmental officers for the purpose of administration.

4. Seven departments, namely, foreign or liaison, finance, legal, propaganda, branches, relief, civil, police and intelligence and civil volunteers and four departments for the military, namely, war, recruits, military intelligence, military police and prisoners of war, were to be organised.

5. It was resolved that if, at the discretion of the Council of Action, it would be feasible to convene a meeting of the representatives and take their advice on the matter of general policy, the Council shall do so.

It was further resolved that before taking any military action against India, including Ceylon (now Sri Lanka), contrary to the wishes, policy or opinion of the Indian National Congress, the Council of Action shall first get the approval of the committee of representatives and act as directed.

The members of the meeting made the following request to the Japanese government: "We request that military action against India will be taken only by the Indian National Army and under the command of Indians together with such military, naval and air co-operation and assistance as may be requested from the Japanese authorities by the Council of Action.

They further requested the government of Japan to make a formal declaration to the following effect:

a. That Japan is ready and willing to give all possible help to India to sever its connection from the British empire and attain complete independence;

b. That on such severance of India from the British empire, Japan would recognise the full sovereignty of India on attaining independence;

c. That absolute independence of India would be guaranteed by the government of Japan;

d. That the government of Japan would exercise its influence with other powers and induce them to recognise the independence and sovereignty of India; and

e. That the framing of the future constitution of India will be left entirely to the representatives of the people of India.

It was resolved by the conference to request the government of Japan to render such financial help for successfully carrying out the object as may be required from time to time on the distinct understanding that such help should be treated as a loan to be repaid to Japan by the national government of independent India when it comes into being as also to give all facilities for propaganda, travel, transport and communication within the area under the control of the Japanese government in the manner and to the extent requested by the Council of Action and also provide all facilities to come into contact with the national leaders, workers and organisations in India.

The Japanese government was further requested to clarify the position of Indian troops then under control (Japanese) in occupied territories, and to recognise and facilitate the use of the national flag of India in all territories under their control. And, in all matters of administration affecting the Indian community, they were to consult the Indian Independence League of the respective places and where there were no League branches recognised leaders of the community approved by the League branch in such places.

The conference resolved that the next conference be held in Bangkok, in the third week of May 1942 and that representatives from the various territories attend the meeting. Seats were allotted as follows – eight each for Japan, Shanghai, Hong Kong, Borneo and Java; twenty each for Malaya and Burma; nine for Thailand; five for Indo-China and two for Manila and Macao and all added up 90 seats. The Indian National Army in East Asia was also to send an equal number of representatives.

Finally, the conference committed itself to a definite policy for the closest co-operation with Japan after obtaining an official definition of the term 'Greater East Asia Co-prosperity Sphere' and its implications.

The conference recorded its profound gratitude to the government of Japan for its active support and sympathy for the cause of Indian independence and for the ample facilities provided for the successful conclusion of the conference. It also recorded profound thanks to Rash Beharl Bose who by tact, patience and geniality as chairman contributed no little to the success of the conference.

The Bangkok Conference

The Indian Independence Conference was held in Bangkok from 15 to 23 June 1942 and not in the third week of May as decided earlier in Tokyo. The delay was mainly due to the difficulty in bringing together the various representatives from the scattered areas. While civil transport facilities were either destroyed or damaged by the war, Japanese military transports – by air, sea and land – were made available to all delegates who reached Bangkok on or before 14 June.

Some 112 delegates, including representatives of the Indian Army (prisoners of war) in Malaya and Hong Kong, attended the conference. They came from Japan, Manchuko, Shanghai, Hong Kong, Borneo, Java, Malaya, Burma, Thailand and the Philippines. The reception and accommodation of the delegates were handled by A.M. Nair and Lt. Itto of the Japanese army secret service, and they did a good job. They spared neither money nor effort to give comfort to their guests from near and far off places in East Asia. Rash Behari Bose received groups of delegates or delegations from the various territories separately and in groups. There were many dinner and tea parties. The Indians in Bangkok too entertained the delegates spending lavishly for their numerous guests. And the visitors were happy and naturally elated. They were all accommodated in high-class hotels in Bangkok, the majority in the French hotel – The Trocodoro Hotel – where Rash Behari Bose and his colleagues from Japan established themselves early with the convenient Room No. 18 as a temporary office.

The delegates to the conference were 'selected,' 'collected' and 'elected' from the various territories they came from. Here, I am tempted to give some details of my journey to Bangkok and my experiences there.

I was the secretary-general of the 'Free Federation of Indians' in Kuching, Borneo. On 18 May 1942, the commander of the Japanese garrison in Kuching sent for me with a message that there was something urgent. At his residence, he told me that there was going to be a conference of Indians in Bangkok on 15 June, and that I should take with me four members of our organisation and proceed to Bangkok via Miri-North Borneo. He wanted me to take with me some good spiritual leaders. I told him it was not possible, and then he told me to select the best men I know. I selected four people.

Indians in Kuching, men, women and children, all gathered to send us off. It was an unprecedented gathering of the Indian community that bid us farewell at the Kuching wharf on the afternoon of 18 May 1942. Most of the senior officers of the Japanese army in that area too were there to see us off. We sailed to Miri in a small battleship. After a short stay there, we left to Saigon by a Japanese military plane – a bomber. Some interesting events at Saigon are worth mentioning. We were put up at a motel infested with Japanese secret service men. A lieutenant by name Hamasaki who received us at the airport told us that he was on special duty to look after the accommodation and transport of the Borneo delegates on their way to Bangkok. He spoke good English. But, later,

I learned from him that he could speak Hindustani, Bengali, Tamil and a bit of Malayalam. He became a friend and he told us a lot about the Japanese, which none in those days dared to talk.

We arrived at a hotel, the name of which I do not recollect, at about 9.00 p.m. Rash Behari Bose and his colleagues were in that same hotel. But the Japanese took good care that we did not meet him or any of his aides. Early next morning the Indians from Japan left for Bangkok by plane. After their departure, a Japanese colonel introduced himself and started to talk to me about India and Indian leaders. I remained a listener all through. He spoke about Rash Behari Bose and added that Bose was a Japanese subject and was there in Japan for over 28 years. He, however, gave the name of A.M. Sahay, who he said was the most suitable person to lead the Indian independence movement. As I knew nothing about both of them then, I simply said that unless I knew about them, I was not competent to give my views regarding the leadership. I thanked him for the tip. Later, I learnt that the Japanese officer was a friend of A.M. Sahay and was deputed to divide the Indians into two groups at least.

We stayed for some days in Saigon merely for want of transport, and left for Bangkok on 3 June 1942, by train, and reached there on the sixth of the month. We were accommodated in the Eagle Hotel from where we shifted to the Trocodero Hotel after four days.

Rash Behari Bose, who presided over the meetings, appointed a preparatory committee to chalk out the various details of the conference. Col Gill dominated the scene all through with his powerful personality and pleasing manners. It should be remembered that he was prominent at the Tokyo Conference as well.

The conference started with an open session at the Silpakorn Theatre Hall in Bangkok from 9.00 a.m. to 1.00 p.m. on 15 June 1942 with N. Raghavan in the chair.

The Indian national anthem was followed by silent prayer for the martyrs of the Indian independence movement. The message to the conference from His Excellency the Premier of Thailand was read out in the meeting. The chairman of the reception committee, D.N. Das, made a welcome speech. Rash Behari Bose was then elected unanimously as the president of the Indian Independence League, East Asia. He addressed the meeting in Hindustani. The English translation of the speech was distributed among the audience.

Address by Rash Behari Bose

Your excellencies, friends and compatriots,

Allow me to express my sincere thanks for the great honour you have bestowed on me by calling upon me to occupy this chair and guide the deliberations of this historic conference.

While greatly appreciating this expression of love and affection for me, I am not unaware of the fact that along with this honour you have put a great responsibility on my shoulders by electing me the president of the conference. However, if I have obeyed your command and taken this chair in spite of the intricacies of the problems, it is because of my great faith in your spirit of co-operation and your sincere desire to put your heads together and come to useful decisions without wasting much of your time on unnecessary discussions and arguments. I am sure I can count on your unreserved help and cooperation in successfully conducting the business of the conference.

As I stand here my thought goes to the unfortunate air accident last March that claimed the lives of our four valuable comrades – Swami Satyananda Puri and Gyani Pritam Singh of Bangkok, and Captain Akram and Sri Neelakanda Ayer of Malaya – while they were flying to Tokyo to attend the Indian Independence Conference. We can well realise the great loss to our cause at such an important period of our struggle and we all feel it very deeply.

However, brethren, let us take it as inevitable, and pray for the peace of their souls. In our grim final struggle against British imperialism, we shall have to offer great sacrifices. Many of us will have to lay down our lives before the world can see India free. It can be well said that these four comrades have given us the lead of which our compatriots in Thailand and Malaya can be proud of.

During and since 1857, when we first revolted against British imperialism in India, hundreds of thousands of our most respected and beloved compatriots have laid down their lives in their struggle to free our motherland. We cannot forget the fact that they nourished the seeds of Swaraj with their blood, and it is the result of their supreme sacrifices that we are today so near our goal and can hope with confidence to achieve independence in the near future.

World knows only a few in the long list of those Indian victims of British imperialism. Let us pay respect to the memory of those known and unknown comrades. Today, placed as we are, very little can be done beyond that. But the time is fast approaching when in every city and town in India we shall find a worthy monument erected in their memory and we Indians will be paying our respectful homage to their memory and look upon them with pride, worthy of their great deeds.

Our homage is also due to those organisations, leaders and workers who have in various ways made untiring efforts since 1857 to liberate our country from bondage. Their list is in no way small and in no way their contributions negligible. Let us pay our respects to that greatest living Indian, Mahatma Gandhi, who with his magic wand roused the Indian masses from the centuries-long slumber and created self-confidence in them. We can have no doubt that when the new and true history of India will be written, Mahatma Gandhi's name will be mentioned as the saviour of India.

I do not want to take your time by going into the many details regarding India's struggle for freedom since 1857. Suffice it to say that although the failure of our revolt of 1857 dealt a great blow to the nation and a general depression had overwhelmed the country, our efforts to overthrow British rule never ceased. Under the circumstances prevailing in those days, the activities had to be carried underground and with a limited scope; and whenever there was an opportunity a revolt was attempted. After minor preparatory stages, our first effort on a large scale was made when the Great War of 1914 started. Our workers were active everywhere. The Indian Army was prepared to join the revolt. A part of the Indian Army had actually revolted though rather prematurely. We thought we were going to succeed. Unfortunately we did not meet with success on that occasion. Thousands of our compatriots had to pay the highest price for their patriotism. Thousands were sent to Andamans and Mandalay and hundreds of them remained rotting their lives there forever.

During the World War of 1914–18, the British were partially successful in enlisting India's cooperation by telling lies and making false promises. Our people were misled by the fine twist of tongue of the shrewd British diplomats. They promised us freedom after the War, as they always did. But, soon after the conclusion of that War, Indians realised that the British did not just keep their promise but wanted to take away even that shadow of civil liberty that the Indians were having in pre-War days. When the Indians protested against the infringement on their basic liberties, the response from the British was in the form of bombs, bullets and machine guns. Needless to say the tragedy of the Jallianwala Bagh in

Amritsar in April 1919 is still fresh in the memory of every one of us and that wound has not yet healed. It really cannot be healed until and unless the imperialist forces responsible for the great humiliation are completely destroyed.

Every tragedy, however, has a lesson and so has the tragedy of Jallianwala Bagh. The bloodbath of more than a thousand of those innocent martyrs, that included even women and children, could not go unpunished. The great upheaval that shook India and the great movements of Non-cooperation and Civil Disobedience carried out from one corner to the other across the country were undoubtedly the antitheses of the massacre in Jallianwala Bagh. The Indian National Congress had wonderfully organised the masses of India for political struggle since 1919.

We must bow our heads in reverence to those brothers and sisters who by sacrificing their lives at Jallianwala Bagh had created a new life in India. As we stand today, millions and millions in India are prepared and willing to suffer and sacrifice all for the cause of their motherland.

When in 1939 the War in Europe started, Britain once again began to indulge in jugglery of words in order to secure Indian assistance and help. But, to the great delight of us all, the nationalist leaders in India refused to be misled and had continued to resist all British efforts to drag India into the war. Our respect goes to Mahatma Gandhi for the most admirable way he has led the nation clear of all dangers of getting entangled in this War.

It was against this background in India the Greater East Asia War was declared on 8 December 1941. And, no matter in which part of the world he or she lived, no matter what might be his or her attitude towards Japan, I refuse to believe that there was any true Indian patriot who was not delighted when the news of Japan's declaration of war on the Anglo-Saxon powers reached his ears. I refuse to believe there was any true Indian patriot, whatever be his or her career or conviction, who might have not rejoiced when the mighty Japanese forces on land and sea and in the air went on administering crushing blows to British imperialism in Asia, and their bases in these parts began to totter one after the other like houses of cards. I also refuse to believe there was any one with eyes who was not overjoyed seeing the power of the greatest enemy of humanity and peace, the greatest aggressor of centuries being destroyed? Those of us who were destined to live and work in Japan had particular reasons to be overjoyed at this most welcome happening.

We have been working in Japan for years so that we can see Japan is in a position to stand by the oppressed Asiatics and liberate Asia. We were anxiously awaiting the day when Japan would fully realise the great significance of creating a free and united Asia and would feel convinced that it was in the interest of Japan itself as also for the rest of Asia if not for the world as a whole that the octopus grip of the Anglo-Saxon imperialists in the East is destroyed root and branch. We all were fully convinced that Japan alone was in the position to take the honour. Thus, when, on the morning of that most auspicious day, the day of enlightenment of Lord Buddha, we heard the news of Japan's declaration of war against our common enemy, we felt that our mission in Japan was fulfilled — we felt convinced that India's freedom was assured.

Being in Japan for decades I know well that Japan is not in the habit of talking and debating unnecessary and meaningless things. I know well that she was not in the habit of taking any serious step unless she had fully weighed her *strengths and was convinced of success. I, therefore, did not share the views of those who thought that due to her continued military activities in China she was too exhausted to challenge the mighty Anglo-Saxons or the so-called ABCD combined forces.*

I was one of those who had not the slightest doubt that the war in China was a prelude to the real war against powers that were actually responsible for the continued fratricidal conflict between China and Japan. Moves on the international chess-board during the past ten years or more have been suggesting that such a world-wide conflict was inevitable. It was also apparent that the question of India's freedom could be successfully solved only when Japan rose in arms against British imperialism.

Now that Japan and Thailand have taken up arms against our common foe, the united efforts of our worthy allies ensured the doom of the British empire and our complete victory.

These effective offers on different fronts to destroy our common enemy are a reminder of our own duties and responsibilities in this common effort for our common cause and we must ask ourselves what we have done and what we are going to do to contribute to this great cause. Mere praising of Japan, Italy and Germany will not entitle us to the position for which we are craving. We must contribute our mite and must make the greatest sacrifice we can make. Then alone can we command the respect and co-operation of our worthy allies and then only can we claim a place worthy of a great nation like ours in future international assembly.

Realising this very important fact and our duty towards our motherland at this most important juncture, we in Tokyo promptly met on 8 December 1941 at the Rainbow Grill and decided upon a programme of action. My compatriots formed a committee and asked me to lead the movement and I gladly agreed to abide by their decision. We at first undertook to consolidate Indian opinion in East Asia in favour of a definite fight from without. Meetings were held at different centers in Japan and resolutions passed emphasising the solidarity of our compatriots, the great need of declaring independence of India by destroying British imperialism and expressing confidence in our work.

On 26 December 1941, for the first time in the history of the Indians in Japan, a conference of nearly fifty representatives of the Indians resident in Kobe, Osaka, Yokohama and Tokyo – all the four cities where Indians reside – was held at the Hallway Hotel in Tokyo to consider the problems. A resolution was passed calling upon the Indians to realise the gravity of the situation and the danger ahead of India. The resolution read as follows:

"Whereas the continued defeat of the British and their allies in Europe and Africa has sealed the fate of British imperialists in Europe; whereas the most decisive destruction of British sea and land forces by Japan in the East has given a death blow to the power and prestige of British imperialism in Asia; whereas the war is fast approaching the shores and borders of India, the British stronghold, the Axis Powers may be obliged to invade India in order to destroy the main source of British fighting strength; whereas such an invasion will bring unimaginable and extremely unusual hardships, miseries and sufferings to millions of innocent and helpless Indians in cities, towns and villages; and whereas the only way to avoid this most unhappy situation is to declare complete independence of India from British rule and to cut off all possible connections with British imperialism in all

possible ways immediately, the Indian nationals residing in Japan assembled in this conference most seriously and earnestly appeal to the Indian National Congress and the people of India to immediately declare independence and to capture all power from the British and take immediate effective steps to stop each and every source of Indian aid to British imperialist war and to declare on behalf of the people that India has no desire whatsoever to be involved in this conflict and has never been willing to help Britain.

Our representatives were sent to Shanghai and on 26 January that year a huge gathering of Indian residents of Shanghai was held in Young Men's Association Hall when similar resolutions as passed in Tokyo were very enthusiastically passed and our movement was given unanimous support.

In the meantime, we established contact with the military and civil high commands in Japan and began to impress upon them the necessity of helping India in her struggle for freedom for the achievement of the very object for which Japan has declared war on Britain and America. We made it clear to them that so long as British imperialism in India continued Japan cannot expect a final victory in the war. At last we succeeded in prevailing upon them and General Tojo, the prime minister of Japan, who openly declared before the Imperial Diet that his government was prepared to help the Indians in their efforts to free their country from the long bondage.

In his declaration before the Imperial Diet at the fall of Singapore, he said:

"It is a golden opportunity for India, having as it does several thousand years of history and splendid cultural tradition, to rid herself of the ruthless despotism of Britain

and participate in the construction of the Greater East Asia Co-prosperity Sphere. Japan expects that India will restore its proper status of 'India for the Indians' and it will not stint herself in extending assistance to the patriotic efforts of Indians. Should India fail to awaken to her mission forgetting her history and tradition, and continue as before to be beguiled by the British cajolery and manipulation and act at their beck and call I cannot but fear that an opportunity for the renaissance of the Indian people would be forever lost."

The declaration offered us great encouragement and we felt convinced that India can safely hope to be free before the East Asia war comes to an end. With promise of support from General Tojo, we established our headquarters at Sanno Hotel and started preparations in right earnest. We decided that a conference of the representatives of Indian organisations from the various parts of East Asia should be held for exchanging views regarding our future move. With the help of the military authorities things were conveniently arranged and the representatives of our compatriots residing in Malaya, Hong Kong and Shanghai along with those of us in Tokyo sat in conference for three days and arrived at certain decisions and framed a draft constitution for the working and progress of our movement. These friends from abroad who participated in the Tokyo conference had occasions to come into contact with responsible members of the Japanese army in Tokyo and to know more about the standing of our movement.

Discussions at the Tokyo conference were varied and we did our best to lay down a solid foundation upon which we could base our plan of action in future.

The Tokyo conference was held at a time when things were less settled. Friends from the East Indies were not present. We were deprived of the valuable help and advice of our friends from Thailand due to the unfortunate plane accident. Burma and the Andamans were still in the hands of our enemy. We, therefore, were unable to come to a decision that could be claimed to be representative of the views of our compatriots in East Asia as a whole. We, therefore, decided to hold a larger and more representative conference at a later date when the decisions taken at Tokyo were to be ratified. The assembly in which we all participated that day was also part of the decisions.

The responsibility to convene this conference was placed on my shoulders and I was asked to hold it in the city. The conference was delayed by a couple of weeks. We expected to reach there early but, due to the extraordinary circumstances, things could not always be done as we wanted.

Detailing every event and activity of the four crucial months may not be of much interest to the reader, but it is necessary to acquaint you of what has happened and how. Before we proceed further, a bit of my sentiments which I passed on to my friends at the conference.

Friends,

We all realise the gravity of the situation and also the fact that we are passing through the most important period of India's history. I don't want to waste time on long speeches. We had enough of that during the last more than five decades. We really cannot afford to waste our time on meaningless talks and arguments. Those who want to really serve the motherland cannot have much time to talk. If we go on talking without coming to any concrete decision, time will not wait for us and we shall be left only to shed tears at our past follies. And it will be too late to mend things. I know there are knotty problems that will come before you for discussion and these will need your most careful consideration. I know you will have to do a lot of thinking and clear a lot of doubts before you can decide. But, if you have come with a grim determination to thrash out a positive, concrete and actually useful plan, you will be able to come to quick decisions. Let us all fully realise our responsibilities towards the country of our birth and let us realise that our land cannot afford to lose this golden opportunity that comes only once in centuries. Our brothers and sisters in hundreds of thousands laid down their lives and have suffered and sacrificed for more than a century so that our country may become once again free. Let us rise to the occasion and carry their efforts to success so that the souls of our martyrs in heaven may find peace and be pleased. Let us rise and act so that the great efforts that Mahatma Gandhi made during the last two decades and more may bear fruit and our children in future may think of us with pride and respect as the members of the free nation.

I know many of you have come with doubts and suspicions regarding the ultimate fate of our country as a result of our activities. I can well appreciate your feelings of uncertainly and your desire for security. Yet, I believe they are based on false premise. Having the bitterest experiences of imperialist exploitations for centuries, we have begun to doubt even our good friends and if we insist on this attitude the world will go on and we shall be left behind to regret our indecision.

I want to sound a note of warning here. Our enemy has always been successful in keeping us divided and in creating false impressions in our minds on such occasions. On many occasions in the past we have missed opportunities to free our country by being victims of British propaganda of lies. I can only hope that we shall not repeat our folly. Our doubts and suspicions are to a great extent the result of shrewd and well thought plans of our enemy to sabotage our efforts. Those of us who are intelligent enough and who are not blind to facts and happenings can see the way clearly.

We should be thankful to the governments of Japan, Germany, Thailand and Italy for the friendly attitude they have been showing toward our cause. We must be particularly thankful to Japan for the most encouraging, definite and helpful promise to help in our sacred cause. Let us not forget the words of Jawaharlal Nehru: "Success often comes to those who dare and act: it seldom goes to the timid."

I make an earnest appeal to you all friends to see that when you conclude your session you have a most practical and workable plan of action for India's freedom so that we can start our work right after the conference and march ahead. We are fortunate enough to have the most valuable help of the Indian National Army which is at our disposal. They deserve our great respect for the great service they have already rendered to our cause by refusing to serve the enemies of India. No one can doubt the bravery of our soldiers in a righteous fight for a righteous cause.

Our sympathies go to the families and friends of those Indian soldiers who had, erroneously believing that they have been fighting for a right cause, lost their lives in Europe and Asia. They have been misled by the same propaganda of lies by Britain that is responsible for the unfounded suspicion in the minds of so many of us. I bow my head to our brave soldiers. We should have no doubt that with their whole-hearted support we are going to win our fight against British imperialism. Let us stand shoulder to shoulder and let us march hand in hand to success. Let us remember we have one indivisible nation – India, one enemy – England, one goal – complete independence.

—Bande Mathram

This was followed by speeches by A.K. Sahay and Captain Mohan Singh in Hindustani and N. Raghavan and Col Gill in English. Their excellencies the ambassador of Japan and the ministers of Germany and Italy also addressed the gathering. The open session concluded at 11.00 p.m.

The second meeting was held the next day and subsequent meetings went on till 23 June 1942, with Rash Behari Bose in the chair. The resolutions passed were more or less the same as those passed at the Tokyo conference. A Council of Action with five members was elected with Rash Behari Bose as its president.

The Council members were men of repute like N. Raghavan, Captain Mohan Singh, Col G.Q. Gilani and K.P. Kesava Menon.

N. Raghavan was the popular Indian leader of Malaya. K.P. Kesava Menon was a known member of the Indian National Congress – he was mainly supported by Captain Mohan Singh and his men in the election. Captain Mohan Singh, the GOC of the Indian National Army, was a brave soldier whose daring won him the love and admiration of many a soldier and whose very name was a by-word for bravery for the Indians in East Asia. Col G.Q. Gilani was the choice of Mohan Singh.

The major decisions of the conference were:

- To organise the Indians in East Asia into an Indian Independence League that would strive for India's independence;

- To raise an Indian National Army from the Indian Army (prisoners of war) as well as from the Indian civilians in East Asia;

- To direct and control the programmes and plan of action of the Indian independence movement so as to bring them in line with the intentions of the Indian National Congress; and

- To demand from the Japanese government further clarification of their policy towards the movement as well as towards India.

These demands made to the Japanese government were clearly drawn out in the form of some twenty-one questions, for which answers were sought by the Council of Action of the Indian Independence League, East Asia and were forwarded through the representative who attended the conference representing the Japanese government.

The headquarters of the Indian Independence League was soon set up and the office started to function in room No. 18 of the Trocodero Hotel in Bangkok.

In accordance with the decisions of the Bangkok Conference, members of the Council of Action were to have their offices at the headquarters of the League. K.P. Keshava Menon was to be in charge of the publicity department, N. Raghavan in charge of administration, Captain Mohan Singh the GOC of the Indian National

Army with Lt. G.Q. Giliani assisting him and Rash Behari Bose as the chief executive and controller of finance.

The members of the Council of Action and some other delegates waited in Bangkok for about a month expecting a reply from the Japanese government. But the reply never came.

One morning, Col Iwakuro, chief of the Japanese office attached to the Indian Independence League (this office was known then as Iwakuro Kikkan) arranged a meeting of the Indian and Japanese representatives. Fifteen Indians, including myself and nine Japanese, were present. There were speeches by Indian and Japanese leaders. Sweet drinks and good cigarettes were served.

Col Iwakuro related an incidence in Japanese and Rash Behari Bose translated the same. It was about a hostel matron, who was kind and considerate. She prepared a good fish curry for a newcomer to the hostel. But the new member did not like fish and liked only meat. The poor old lady's labour was in vain and decided that she would thence forward know what one wanted and then get it prepared. So also the Japanese would do in future. The implication was that the Indians disliked or rather suspected the Japanese for what they have done for the Indians. So the Japanese would thereafter ask the Indians what they wanted and try to serve them. The Bangkok resolutions, Col Iwakuro said, were being studied by his government and the reply would come soon. The meeting ended.

After several meetings, members of the Council of Action left for Malaya. They said they would come back in a month. I went to the railway station to see them off and there N. Raghavan told me that he would never come back to Bangkok. He expressed dissatisfaction and said that things were not what they should be. He wanted me to be alert and inform him privately all about any new developments if any.

Indian Independence League Headquarters Shifted

The Indian Independence League headquarters was shifted from the Trocodero Hotel to 122, Wireless Road, Bangkok. A spacious office building with residential quarters for the president, secretaries and staff was secured by the help of the Japanese.

Many Indians and sons of the delegates were of the opinion that the Bangkok conference was a Japanese show. This was more or less due to A.M. Nair whom most of us considered a typical Japanese. I did not like to work in the headquarters and expressed the same forcefully to B.K. Das who was appointed the general secretary. When I got the letter of appointment as a member of the secretariat, I told Raghavan that I did not like it. I even tore off the letter. I wanted to go with N. Raghavan to Penang to join a school, which he proposed to open there for training volunteers for military and political work in the movement. I liked the idea. But someone informed Rash Behari Bose of my plan and he protested to Raghavan for taking me away with him. And Raghavan persuaded me to stay on in Bangkok for some time and assured to call me over to Penang in a month. But that call never came and I had to be in Bangkok throughout. I left only when the headquarters was shifted to Singapore in March 1943 and I was in charge of that not-too-pleasing job.

Since most of the officers appointed for the headquarters left for Malaya, the Tokyo group assumed charge of the various departments. A.M. Nair was the chief of the show and we used to call him 'Chief of Staff.' A.M. Sahay was the senior member of the secretariat. These men from Japan were a set of happy-go-about people and they took more care of their own pleasures. Most of them consumed much beer and wine. Some of them carried on propaganda against Rash Behari Bose whom they addressed 'Sensay' (chief or leader). They spread the news that Bose was a Japanese subject, was in Japan for thirty years and was a Japanese agent. This created deep suspicion in the minds of a good number among us. We were also surprised at the attitude of Bose towards the Indians from Japan. He trusted them and liked them all.

There were instances of reporting against the workers of the headquarters or members of the League to the Japanese by the Tokyo group. All such reports have been taken seriously by the Japanese who punished them severely. Some of them betrayed their own people for the sake of personal gains or to impress upon the Japanese about their own importance.

The headquarters was a place for holiday making for some of the staff. The publicity and propaganda department under M. Shivaram and S.A. Iyer functioned well. For some time, I worked with them and prepared news and news commentaries in Malayalam that were broadcast over the Bangkok Radio. I kept aloof from the Tokyo group as far as possible, just because I did not like the way in which they behaved. Some of them, particularly A.M. Nair, tried to win me over to their side. They did not succeed. Nair San later became a businessman of repute in Tokyo and a good friend of India in Japan.

With little work to do and the luxury and plenty amidst the war we were having a good time in Bangkok.

Meanwhile, relations between members of the Council of Action and the Japanese were becoming bad in Malaya. The absence of any detailed reply from Tokyo for the Bangkok resolution, the attitude of Iwakuro Kikkan and the apparent unwillingness of the Japanese in the rapid expansion of the Indian National Army were the main causes.

Gen Mohan Singh was a brave soldier but he was not a man of tact. He organised the 20,000-strong Indian National Army, of which he was also the General Officer Commanding. Col N.S. Gill was adviser to Mohan Singh. Now, General Mohan Singh too started doubting the intentions of Rash Behari Bose who he thought was an agent of the Japanese.

Matters came to a head by December 1942. Rash Behari Bose rushed to Malaya to save the situation. The Japanese hoped that he would be able to dissuade the members of the Council of Action from resigning. Rather, he could not. The reply from Tokyo reaffirming Japanese determination to help India win freedom was not the proper reply expected. The situation turned critical on 8 December 1942 with the arrest of Col N.S. Gill in Burma by the Japanese, dubbing him as a British agent or spy. This was done without any prior consultation of the Council of Action or the General Officer Commanding of the Indian National Army. The four members of the Council of Action resigned.

President Rash Behari Bose declared that he would go back to Tokyo and try to get the necessary clarifications on issues from the government in Tokyo and requested that till then the organisation, namely, the League branches, should go on. The members agreed to this on condition that the way forward of the entire movement should be decided only after securing the necessary and desired clarification as well as declarations from the Japanese government.

The Japanese arrested some prominent Indians from Bangkok who were friends of Col Gill, whom they took into custody in Burma.

The Japanese were a peculiar people and the way in which they did things were equally strange. On the morning of 8 December 1942, a Japanese major came to our residence. I had with me seven Indians from Hong Kong who came to join the headquarters. We were having our breakfast at that time. The officer came to our table. We offered him a chair on which he sat down. After drawing a folded file from his pocket, he said, "Sorry, I am going to arrest some of you."

We all were alarmed and struck with fear as he uttered the word, "arrest." After a minute's silence, I took courage to ask him for the list of people he was going to arrest. He gave me the list on which I found neatly typed names of seven prominent Indians in Bangkok.

He took a cup of coffee, thanked us and left. We made inquiries and by evening learned about the arrest of Col Gill and some others in Burma.

It will be of interest to know what actually the Japanese were doing in Burma. They had with them thousands of Indian prisoners of war whom they took to various theatres of war for labour and put to very hard work. From among these men, they selected a few hundred, gave them INA uniforms and badges they prepared and took them to Burma front, in the forefront of their army. Col N.S. Gill, adviser to General Mohan Singh, visited Burma. He was an efficient intelligence officer. He soon learned what the Japanese were doing. In order to fool the people of India, the Japanese were using their puppets in place of INA in the battle, while the Indian National Army remained safe in Singapore. He informed this to his GOC in Malaya. Also, Major Dhillon and a few others who accompanied Gill crossed the border and went to India under the pretext of going for a hunt. The Japanese came to know all these and they soon arrested Col Gill and all his men in Burma. They also arrested intimate friends of that officer in Malaya and Thailand.

General Mohan Singh took a serious view of things when the Japanese arrested Col Gill and others. He demanded immediate release of the arrested men, which the Japanese very politely refused. The Japanese also refused to give transport for the INA to Burma. Mohan Singh consulted K.P. Kesava Menon regarding any steps he were to take. Mohan Singh even came to clash with the president. He called him 'Omachand,' cursed and abused him. He took a bold step and disbanded the INA, which he said was his own army.

These were events quite unexpected and unforeseen by any one and particularly the president, Rash Behari Bose. Had he not been a man of outstanding character and courage he would undoubtedly have given up at this point. But he had realised from early years that the struggle for the freedom of India was bound to be hard and long and was well prepared for disappointments and setbacks. Even those who suspected him to be a Japanese agent admired his sterling qualities. He had great calmness of demeanor, a large amount of firmness and coolness in argument, a pleasant countenance and decided but perfectly gentle manners. Instead, therefore, of allowing himself to lose heart or grow bitter at this major setback, he accepted it as a challenge and became more determined than ever to continue his efforts in carrying on the great movement – the most cherished and dearest of his ambitions – to liberate his motherland from slavery and bondage. He remained wonderfully calm and level headed.

On 10 December 1942, Rash Behari Bose appealed to the Indians in East Asia; his appeal in pamphlet form was sent to all League branches in East Asia. As it gives details of all the important developments, the statement as such is given below:

Brethern,

It has been my desire for some time to clear the existing misunderstanding between the Indian National Army and the Indian Independence League. But, unfortunately, owing to the extremely heavy pressure of work, I have not been able to express my views in public, although I did manage to talk to the military officers and civilian officials of the League. Later, I wish to speak before a mass meeting on the whole issue, but for the present wish to circulate this statement for your immediate information.

It is a known fact that our motherland has been exploited and looted by the British for the last two centuries and during this period thousands of our patriots and leaders have sacrificed their lives for the emancipation of Hindustan. Even today thousands of our brethren in India are being murdered daily. This is the reason that not only in India but all over the world every Indian is clamouring for the freedom of India. Remember the words of our leader Mahatma Gandhi "Do or Die."

It is about thirty years ago that I threw a bomb at the viceroy and as I was an active member of the Lahore, Delhi and Banarus conspiracies. I had to leave my country and seek foreign help. With the aid of Germany I was able to send home two shiploads of arms and ammunitions but unfortunately they were confiscated before reaching India. What was the motive behind all this?... Freedom of my country, which is very dear to me. I feel confident that every one of you has the same love for the freedom of our fair land, if not more. As for me, I have forsaken everything in life — wealth, relatives and all other things which were dear to me — for the sake of my country. The British offered thousands of rupees as reward for my head. They succeeded in persuading the Japanese government through their ambassador to hand me over to them, and I was ordered by the Japanese government to leave Japan within five days. But, fortunately, some of my Japanese friends let me stay in obscurity in their houses for seven years. Had the British been successful in taking me back to India I would have been killed long ago. That is why I have great belief in Almighty God who has helped me and guided me all through these perilous years and I hope he will not forsake me in this sacred work, which you have placed on my shoulders by electing me as the president of the Council of Action at the Bangkok conference. I shall see that our mission does not fail, and the trust put in me is faithfully carried out.

Comrades, let me tell you that we in the Far East shall soon join hands with our brethren at home and shall create such a resolution in India that we will achieve our most cherished purpose of complete freedom of India. Be ready to die as free men rather than live as slaves. The time has passed for India to stay under a foreign power. India must be free during this struggle. India would have been free long ago if we were in possession of arms and ammunition. History tells us that many nations have fought their battles with foreign help. In our struggle for independence, the more the Congress fought with non-violent methods the more brutal became the methods of the British. For this reason I worked in Japan with a view to asking for help when the occasion arose. I am glad to tell you that my work and labour of the last thirty years have borne fruit.

At the outbreak of the Greater East Asia War, I interviewed the minister of home affairs and other important officials of various departments, as well as members of the general staff in Japan, with a view to securing their support and co-operation in our struggle for freedom, and I was promised such support. "I can assure you that in Japan you will find a true and sympathising friend. She has very clear intentions about the independence of India. The help she is offering to Indians is not because she wants to dominate India but because the enemies of India were also her enemies, and, therefore, co-operation and unity between the two peoples was essential," he said.

"I can tell you that Japan will not rest until the last soldier of Anglo-Saxon race is removed from India, she is determined to destroy British-American influence in Asia, so why should we not grasp this God-sent opportunity and fight for the complete freedom of India?"

"Before I go any further, I want to say very clearly that the Indian independence movement is ours and ours alone, which *is specifically formed to fight for the independence of India. Remember this movement is neither of the Japanese people nor of their government. They have nothing whatsoever to do with it except that they have offered all their help for the defeat of the common foe, for which we are indeed grateful. But, if a time were to come when we begin to receive not sufficient help or say nothing at all, should we give up our movement? The answer is 'No.' The movement should continue until our country is completely free from any kind of foreign domination or influence. It is our movement, our struggle and we alone have the power to decide its fate.*

It is, therefore, imperative for every true son of India who loves freedom to join this movement heart and soul and move forward with complete determination until our independence is achieved. We all know we would have to face several drawbacks, disappointments, difficulties and obstructions in the attempt but should not be disheartened as we have shouldered a most sacred cause and have become the custodians of the four hundred millions of India. We are duty-bound to see that the movement is not used by anyone for any other purpose, except for gaining India's independence. It is the duty of every one of us to be ready to crush any opposition even in the face of death in this attempt.

Remember that at the declaration of the Greater East Asia War, the Indian independence movement was at full swing in Japan, Shanghai, Canton and Bangkok. The Indian Independence League was established by me in Japan in 1924. I was fully aware of the position of Indians during and after the war and I had a clear understanding with the Japanese government in this matter. It was through this process that Major Fujiwara asked for the co-operation of Indian patriots and our late beloved Sardar Pritam Singh took a major part in the pageant of the Malay campaign.

Captain Mohan Singh joined hands with Sardar Pritam Singh on 12 December 1941. Fujiwara, being a Japanese officer, did not know very much about the Indian soldiers and so the administration and command of Indian military personnel was given over to Capt. Mohan Singh. It was desired that they be taught the virtues of nationalism, patriotism and love for freedom and prepare them for the struggle for the freedom of India.

I realised that the organisation of the independence movement in East Asia was not merely my affair but the concern of all my countrymen residing here. It was for this reason that I arranged for a conference of some of the leaders in East Asia, including military officers, which was held in Tokyo in March last year.

The fundamental principles of this movement were laid down at that conference. Subsequently, at the Bangkok conference, I received the mandate of our countrymen in East Asia to carry on this movement in the best way possible. Considerable progress has been made in the great work we have undertaken and in this Capt. Mohan Singh has played a major part. There are great possibilities of our succeeding in attaining our objective.

The Bangkok conference was held in June last year and certain resolutions were passed for the guidance and working of the movement. In accordance with these resolutions, a Council of Action was elected as the supreme executive body of the movement.

Prior to the election, Capt. Mohan Singh, in his speech, made some statements, which now appear to be misrepresentation of facts because he solemnly gave us to understand that the majority of the Indian Army personnel were prepared to join this movement without any threat of force and that they had acclaimed him as their military leader. I was horrified at a later date to learn of the atrocities meted out to officers and men of the Indian Army for which the blame naturally falls on Capt. Mohan Singh. Many of our poor brethren were shot while many were threatened with violence. He demoralised the majority of officers and men and compelled them to become volunteers, which is against our principle. I for one would be the last man to see my countrymen shot in cold blood. This is what we are fighting for against the British and I personally cannot afford to see Indians tortured in this manner.

In accordance with the resolutions of the Bangkok Conference, the Indian National Army was part of the Indian Independence League and all officers and men of the INA owed allegiance to the League. It must be understood that an army is an army of a country and not of an individual. So it was wrong for INA personnel to give allegiance to an individual without raising objections. I was under the impression that the INA as a whole was well aware of the resolutions because an officer was purposely sent down as a representative of Capt. Mohan Singh to explain in detail the resolutions to the army, which I understand, he did from camp to camp. Not only that, I am also given to understand that on return of Capt. Mohan Singh, a few conferences were held at his bungalow and the position was clarified to the officers who later joined the INA.

I, however, was being informed of the situation in Singapore and I felt it desirable to hold a meeting of the Council of Action in Bangkok. But, unfortunately, the members could not present themselves for some reason or the other. And, under the circumstances, I was forced to come to Syonan for discussions.

There was never, at any moment, any divergence of opinion on the broad principles along which this movement should continue, nor were there any differences of opinion as to the necessity of obtaining sufficient assurances from the imperial government of Japan regarding their acceptance of the basic principles enunciated at the Bangkok Conference. The reply to the Bangkok resolutions, which was delivered to us on 10 July, was not very satisfactory. I was in agreement with my colleagues that a further clarification of the imperial government's attitude towards the resolutions adopted at the Bangkok conference was desirable. On 5 September 1942, we sent a letter to Colonel Iwakuro requesting that the imperial government should give us a more elaborate reply to the Bangkok resolutions. On receipt of this letter, Col Iwakuro informed me that such a request to the imperial government might be misconstrued and may lead to a good deal of misunderstanding and suggested that the letter be withdrawn. The Council of Action held an emergency meeting on 7 September, at which all members except Raghavan were present. The meeting decided to withdraw the letter and it was done accordingly.

This matter again came up for a good deal of discussion in the meetings of the Council of Action during the later part of November. The necessity for requesting a further clarification of the imperial government's attitude on these important issues was found essential. We, therefore, formulated our proposals and submitted them to Col Iwakuro for forwarding it to the imperial government of Japan and, at a joint conference, we explained to Col Iwakuro the necessity of giving us more formal assurances than we had up till then.

Although the discussion with Col Iwakuro did not give us full satisfaction, I pleaded with my colleagues in the Council of Action that they should give me time to take up these important issues with the imperial government of Tokyo. On 20 November, the Council of Action decided that my colleague, N. Raghavan, and I should visit Tokyo if needed and take up these important matters directly with the Tokyo government.

In the later part of November, it came to light that Capt. Mohan Singh as GOC of the INA had arranged with the Iwakuro Kikkan for the transport of some INA troops to Burma for purpose of training. The GOC sent an advance party to Rangoon without the consent of the Council of Action. Naturally, the Council wished to know about the move in great detail and was not prepared to sanction movement of troops without its knowledge. During the discussions in the Council of Action, Capt. Mohan Singh, for the first time since the Bangkok conference, placed before the Council the state of affairs existing in the Army. It was then that the Council of Action came to realise that if the Indian National Army was to become a strong and efficient fighting force for achieving our freedom, a radical change in the existing organisation was long overdue.

It is perhaps essential to state here the reasons why I, as president of the Council of Action, left all questions relating to the Indian National Army in the hands of Capt. Mohan Singh. I was of the opinion before these facts became known to us that it would be better to entrust the organisation of the INA in the hands of our GOC and give him the necessary confidence. The Council must refrain from interfering with the work of the GOC in the belief that the latter would, in turn, keep the Council totally informed of the position of the Indian National Army from time to time.

There have been ample opportunities for the GOC to apprise the Council during its sittings in September and

October of all the difficulties that he was facing in relation to the organisation of the INA. But, unfortunately, in these matters, either no information or very meager information was supplied to the Council of Action.

I regret to have to say that in matters connected with the INA, the GOC arrived at important decisions without referring to the Council of Action. In fact, the Council was kept almost in the dark regarding the various important activities of the INA – a state of affairs which we tried to rectify. I thought it was vitally important that the Council of Action should immediately take control of the policy regarding the Army and all questions of major importance should be decided by the Council and not by the GOC. I had to write to Col Iwakuro to that effect so that no further mistakes would be committed.

Because of this muddle, which could have been avoided, Raghavan who was all the time advocating better co-ordination between the Army and the Council, resigned. I requested him to withdraw his resignation as matters were getting better. On 4 December, at my request, members of the Council agreed to give me time till the end of January 1943, to enable me to obtain full and satisfactory assurances from the Japanese government. I was glad that I was given further time to attempt a solution to these difficult questions before my colleagues resigned.

The next morning, that is, on 5 December, I was surprised to hear from Capt. Mohan Singh, Col Gilani and K.P. Keshava Menon that notwithstanding the previous day's decision, they were not prepared to carry on the movement unless an assurance was immediately given that a reply to the Bangkok resolutions in detail would be obtained on or before 1 January 1943. As far as I know, there was no one *in Malaya capable of giving such an assurance. Moreover, it was virtually an ultimatum to the Japanese government, which would have offended them. I then realised that an attempt was being made to obstruct an issue-based solution of the questions in order to wreck the movement. This I was not prepared to agree to. I was not then, and even till today, satisfied that the Japanese government was prepared to help the movement in such a manner as we desired. If we find they were not sincere, then we would stop seeking their help, but not until then.*

Notwithstanding the inexplicable attitude of my colleagues, I tried to negotiate with the Japanese authorities to arrive at a formula, which would help us in tiding over the crisis.

On 8th December, a most unfortunate event happened – the Japanese authorities arrested Col Gill for certain investigations. Col Gill had taken an active part in the present crisis. However, on enquiry, I found out that his arrest had no connection with our crisis, although it gave such an impression.

On the afternoon that day, a meeting of the Council of Action was convened, when Raghavan was absent. However, the other members insisted that unless their request for sending an ultimatum on 5th December were acceded to immediately, it would be impossible for them to continue in the movement. The meeting was adjourned till 10th December for further discussions on all the issues.

Later, in the evening, however, I received a letter of resignation signed by all the three of them. I must confess that it did not cause much surprise to me because I had a feeling for some time that they were not interested in attempting a settlement. So I accepted all the resignations. This being the position, I had no other alternative but to take over the powers and duties of the entire Council of Action according to our constitution, pending election of new members, which can be done only at a meeting of representatives of various territories in East Asia and the Indian National Army.

Capt. Mohan Singh, from the very beginning, wanted to carry on his work despotically. He wanted to have a free hand in whatever he undertook and, as such, he could not bear the idea of being interfered with by others in his work. But, constitutionally, he had to work under the Council of Action. In order to overcome this restriction, he intensified his exercise of dictatorial influence over the INA and infused wrong ideas in the minds of his officers and men that the army belonged to him, and that he was the master.

Moreover, at the last meeting of the Council of Action, Capt. Mohan Singh tried to blot out the Council of Action pressing upon the Council to get immediate clarifications on a few questions from the Japanese authorities, which, as I have stated above, was impossible because there was none in Malaya who could answer on the spot. On receiving no reply, he, as well as the other two members of the Council of Action tendered their resignations the same evening without waiting to meet on 10th December, as previously arranged. Col Gillani, in his capacity as an officer of the INA under Mohan Singh, had no alternative but to comply with the wishes of his superior and thus relinquished his post.

Since Capt. Mohan Singh was instrumental in the election of Mr. Menon as a member of the Council of Action and his election was mainly due to the military votes, he was obliged to resign along with Mohan Singh.

Two of the highest military officers having resigned, I wished to call the rest of the senior officers in order to acquaint them with the whole situation and inform them of my plans.

So, I asked the GOC to send these officers to meet me at the Sea View Motel on 12th December. The GOC, however, thought it necessary to enquire in what capacity I had called that meeting and what the purpose of that meeting was. As president of the Council of Action, and as such the head of this movement, I was entitled to see any officer of the INA. And the GOC was not at liberty to ask for an explanation from me. However, I pointed out to him that the powers and duties of the Council of Action were vested in me as the president and the sole surviving member of the Council. The GOC not only ignored my directions but, in his letter to me dated 13th December 1942, also stated:

"The members of the Indian National Army are pledged to me (ie, Captain Mohan Singh) and me alone by name"; and, "Under the existing circumstances, we (meaning, I presume, the Army) cannot usefully serve our motherland through the Indian Independence League in East Asia and have accordingly thought it fit to sever our connection with it.

The tone and contents of this letter came to me as a great shock. I could hardly imagine that any officer appointed GOC of any army would disown the very movement of which the army forms an integral part and claim that the army is his own private personal army. I could not for a moment believe that any officer or say men who had volunteered for service in the INA did ever imagine that he was pledging loyalty to an individual and not to the movement which brought in the existence of that army.

When Capt. Mohan Singh resigned from the membership of the Council of Action and said that he had nothing to do with this movement, he should naturally have washed his hands of the command of the INA. But he did not. He waited for a further three weeks, thinking that the Council of Action does not exist, and that any decision reached between the Indian side and the Japanese would be between him and the Japanese government. But his idea did not materialise as the Japanese authorities struck to the Bangkok resolution by recognising the Council of Action as the supreme body of which I was the only surviving member. In fact, Capt. Mohan Singh had approached Col Iwakuro with a letter stating clearly that the Indian National Army belonged to him and that he wished to dissolve it. On the other hand, he informed his officers that if anything happened to him they should dissolve the army immediately.

On the face of it, I had to take the most painful but the only available course of action, namely, the removal of Gen Mohan Singh from his post as GOC of the Indian National Army.

Before closing the facts of the case, I want to give you extracts from the speeches of the Japanese Premier General H. Tojo on various occasions concerning India and from which I hope you will be able to know the attitude of the Japanese government towards India.

In his address before the Diet on the fall of Singapore on 16 February 1942, Premier General Tojo said:

"It is a golden opportunity for India, having as it does several thousand years of history and splendid cultural tradition, to rid herself of the ruthless despotism of Britain and participate in the construction of the Greater East Asia Co-prosperity Sphere. Japan expects that India will restore its proper status as India for the Indians and it will not stint herself from extending assistance to the patriotic efforts of the Indians. Should India fail to awaken to her mission forgetting her history and traditions and continue as before to be beguiled by British cajolery and manipulation and act at their beck and call, I cannot but fear that an opportunity for the renaissance of the Indian people would be forever lost."

In his message to the Imperial Diet on 12 March 1942 the Premier said:

It is my firm belief that now is the time to establish India for the Indians, which has for many years been the aspiration of the 400 million Indian people. Great Britain has for long deceived and continued her arbitrary rule over India. The reality of the British promise made to India in the last Great War must be still fresh, I believe, in the memory of the Indian people. Now Great Britain is trying again to deceive India with all sorts of cajolery. If the leaders of India, misled by such British cajoleries, betray the long cherished aspiration of the Indian people and thus fling away this heaven send opportunity, I believe, there will be no chance for saving India ever and there will be no greater misfortune befalling the 400 million Indian people.

Will India rise as India for the Indians and have the honour to co-operate for the establishment of the Great East Asia Co-prosperity Sphere, or will she permanently stoop under the shackles of the Anglo-American powers to leave her name as a slave to posterity? She is now face to face with the time, when she should liquidate her past, see the new situation correctly and make her final decision.

In his advice to India on 7 April 1942, General Tojo said:

The imperial forces which previously occupied Rangoon, an important base in Burma, and then took possession of the more strategic point in the eastern Indian Ocean, the Andaman Islands, which has hitherto been a place of exile for patriots fighting for Indian independence, have now at last dealt severe blows to the British forces and military establishments in India.

The grim determination of our Empire to crush the United States and Britain is thus being steadily translated into action. If India should remain as before under the military control of Britain, it would, I am afraid, be unavoidable that, in course of our subjugation of the British forces there, India will suffer great calamities.

It is farthest from the thought of Japan to consider the Indian people as an enemy, and Japan deeply sympathises with them who are likely to suffer the ravages of war.

What Japan's intentions are towards the Indian people were made clear in my address delivered before the Imperial Diet on 12 March (see above). In short, I am firmly convinced that now is the golden opportunity for the Indian people to exert their utmost efforts in order to secure India's status as it ought to be.

The British influence in India is now about to be exterminated. I wish once again to repeat at this juncture Japan's expectation that not only the leaders in India but the four hundred million people there, while avoiding unnecessary calamities, which will result from their being misled by sweet flatteries of Britain, the nation destined to downfall, will take full advantage of this heaven-sent opportunity and break away from the British bonds, which have so long shackled them and thus go vigorously forward to realise truly their long cherished aspiration of "India for the Indians."

In his address before the Lower House of the Diet on the progress of war and the economic problems of Greater East Asia on 28 May 1942, Premier Tojo said:

"There still remains in India a framework of British possession with various military establishments, and the military forces are being steadily increased. As long as there remain

Anglo-American military forces in India, Japan is determined inflexibly to crush them thoroughly. To our regret, it is, indeed unavoidable that in the progress of such campaign, some misfortunes may befall innocent Indians. What I expect at this juncture, however, is that the Indian people will rise with an intrepid spirit, expel the Anglo-American forces as well as their influence completely from India and thereby realise the independence of their Fatherland."

I must emphasise that before we can take a final and decisive step to completely stop this movement, we have got to be satisfied beyond doubt that the Japanese authorities are not sincere in their desire to assist us and that they want to use us as mere fifth-columnists or puppets. It is also necessary before the final step is taken to consider the repercussions of such a step on the two and half million Indians in East Asia and 400 million in India, a matter which seems to have escaped the attention of my three colleagues. I would have been untrue to the trust reposed in me by you all if I had allowed any wrecking of the movement immediately and before we could even find out the attitude of Tokyo.

I have given you a true description of the whole situation and I leave it to your good judgment to decide. You must always remember that this movement and the Army do not belong to any one man and they can never be so. The foundation of this movement was laid years ago. Despite all opposition to the struggle, it is gaining momentum. Many die in the struggle and a greater number take their place. Many have played their part in this struggle for India's freedom and disappeared from the stage in sacrifice but the movement continues to expand as it carries us towards the ultimate goal. I may die tomorrow, but one of you should be ready to take my place and when he dies there should be another to take over the responsibilities. It is the most sacred duty of every

Indian to sacrifice his all for the complete independence of India and the Hindustan of tomorrow will be proud of you. If you survive in the struggle, you shall be called heroes and if you die in the attempt you shall be martyrs.

I, therefore, appeal to you in the name of our Motherland to set aside all petty differences, make one unit of brotherhood and move forward as one team, and the freedom of our country is assured. Remember, you are born only once and will die only once, whether it is in a sick bed or on the battlefield. Come forward as men, live as men, so that the India of tomorrow can be proud of you.

The Indian National Army does not belong to me or Mohan Singh or to any one of you but it is the vision of four hundred million Indians. Remember, when it did not exist it did not exist, but once it is formed, see that nobody can break it. It shall only break when no trace of an enslaved India is left. If you have the feeling of nationalism and want to live as free citizens of the world, then answer the call of your motherland and join the movement. By serving your country, you are serving yourself. A small party of true and patriotic men is worth more than an army of hundred thousand which may betray India at the time of her need.

Comrades, it is a God-sent opportunity. Everything is in our favour. One of the world's greatest powers is prepared to help us. And even the inner voice of the heart tells me that India must be free during this struggle.

Inquilab Zindabad!

Rash Behari Bose interviewed senior officers of the disbanded INA separately and in groups and reorganised the army with great difficulty. This army was different; it was controlled and administered by a committee called the Military Bureau. Col Bhonsle was director of this bureau and Lt. Col M.Z. Khaini was appointed the Army Commander. Some of the ardent and faithful followers of Gen Mohan Singh refused to join the new INA, but the majority, more than 12,000 officers and men, joined. Those who refused were taken away to Sumatra Island by the Japanese. They also arrested and took into custody some of the leaders of the group who were against joining the INA. The situation was thus brought under control in the British style.

Col Iwakuro issued a statement in which he expressed surprise at the resignation of the members of the Council of Action. He praised Mohan Singh's bravery and patriotism but regretted his lack of understanding and good sense. Soon, the Iwakuro Kikkan started to set up a parallel organisation to weaken the Indian Independence League, or perhaps to have one under their control. Notorious youth leaders like K.K.K. Menon and S. Rajaram of Singapore played into the hands of the Japanese for some time. But it was not at all successful. Rash Behari Bose supported the youth movement only as part of the Indian Independence League and under its control. He, therefore, instructed all League branches to open a youth section as well as a women's section. He thus foiled the attempt of Iwakuro Kikkan to divide the Indians. Rajaram and K.K.K. Menon also carried on propaganda against Raghavan and other leaders of the Indians in Malaya. This too was of no use and so these radicals finally joined the Indian Independence League. The Japanese learnt well that they cannot fool the Indians for long.

Rash Behari Bose decided to bring the headquarters to Singapopre. And, according to his instructions, the packing of all the furniture and stores belonging to the Indian Independence League headquarters was completed by 24 March 1943. I was in charge of this arduous task, being the general secretary then. I left Bangkok with the goods in a special goods train, which brought me to Singapore on 28 March 1943.

The evening of 28 March 1943 is very fresh in my memory. That evening, I called on the president in order to give him the list of furniture and stores I brought from Bangkok. He was alone in his room. Contrary to his habit, he came out to receive me. He looked pale and the hand he extended to me was weak. Within two months' time, he seemed to have grown older by ten or fifteen years. He took his seat and asked me to take the seat opposite to him. His servant brought us tea and after tea he offered me a cigarette, which I politely declined. Straight away, instead of asking me anything about my trip in the goods train from Bangkok to Singapore or anything personal, he said Subhash Chandra Bose would be coming to take up the leadership of the Indian independence movement. I did not believe him and remained silent. I saw tears in his eyes.

He said and I quote: "VNK, you are still thinking that I am a Japanese agent. It is not your fault. I know it for long. Please do believe this old man, I am the last Indian to be a Japanese agent. I will die happily rather than do disservice to our motherland, India." He stood up, I followed and he embraced me as an old father his son. Tears fell on my collar and it flowed down from there. I was suddenly in tears. He asked me to go if I desired. I did not go. I told him frankly that I took him for a Japanese spy. I admitted that I was wrong and misinformed and begged his pardon. He said nothing but gently patted me on my shoulder.

We sat down again. He asked me about things in Bangkok and all about my trip and the stores I brought. He said I looked tired and asked me whether I had a friend in upcountry Malaya with whom I could stay and rest for a while. I suggested a place in lower Perak where I had my own niece. In fact, I wanted to go there. He agreed to get me passage and necessary permits to go there but wanted me to return as soon as I got his message to do so. I promised and we parted.

In three days' time I got the necessary papers for my travel upcountry. Rash Behari Bose got for me a good suitcase and some pieces of silk as presents to my niece. I was with my relatives for three weeks. Then I got his message to return; to take part in the Singapore conference.

The first conference of Indian Independence League held in Singapore was almost a simple meeting compared with those held at Tokyo or at Bangkok. Early in April 1943, telegrams were sent to all league branches in East Asia to send representatives for the conference. The Japanese authorities arranged transport for the delegates who reached Singapore in time for the conference. Those who came were either the presidents or the secretaries of the various branches and, in a few cases, both these officials came. A Yellappa and Dr. Lukshmayya were presidents of the Singapore and Malaya branches of the Indian Independence League, respectively, and were the prominent actors of the whole show.

The conference was held at the premises of the Singapore branch of the League in Waterloo Street and went on for three consecutive days from 27 April 1943. Rash Behari Bose presided over the meetings and Maj

Gen Iwakuro (he was promoted) attended all the meetings and also made a good speech. I represented Borneo in the conference as there were no representatives from there.

There was nothing new in any of the speeches made by the president, the chairmen of the various League branches and Gen Iwakuro.

The constitution adopted at Bangkok was amended and Rash Behari Bose was made the director of the movement. In the course of their speeches, Dr. Lukshmayya and Barrister Yellappa referred to Rash Behari Bose as the constitution itself. Bose was at that time ill and ailing and of an unhealthy constitution.

In his concluding remarks, Rash Behari Bose announced that Subhas Chandra Bose would succeed him as president and leader of the movement. All were happy.

The headquarters of the League was soon established at No. 7 Chancery Lane, Singapore, more or less in the Bangkok style and with the furniture and stores from there. Lt. Col A.C. Chattarjee was appointed secretary-general and chief liaison officer of the headquarters. Others appointed included Lt. Col Gilani and Lt. Col Loganathan.

Different departments of the league started functioning; the publicity and propaganda department was organised on a large scale and S.A. Iyer and M. Sivaram were busy. On 1 May 1943, the Indian Independence League broadcasting station went on air from Singapore, and two weeks later the Aazad Hind daily was started with M. Sivaram as the chief editor.

The Indian National Army was better organised and more prisoners of war joined the army. Two centres – the

Bharat Youth Training Centre at Kula Lampur and the Azad School at Singapore – started training about 1,500 young men in the art of war. It was decided to impart military training to Indians in East Asia on a large scale.

The president used to visit the office almost daily for a few days but soon the visits became few and far between. His failing health prevented him from this. After posing for a group photograph with the staff of the League headquarters, he left for Tokyo. He reached there in time to receive Netaji Subhas Chandra Bose. He acquainted him with the various problems of the movement. The two were in Tokyo together for two weeks.

Indians everywhere in East Asia were happy to learn about the coming of Netaji and were more enthusiastic than ever to do anything and everything in their power to strengthen the movement. A second conference in Singapore was then urgently convened.

Netaji Comes to Singapore

Netaji arrived in Singapore with Rash Behari Bose and a group of Japanese officials on 2 July 1943. Delegates from all the League branches reached Singapore to hail his arrival. I was in charge of the reception of the delegates from outside Malaya. On 4 July 1943, the Indian representatives assembled at the Cathey Hall to welcome their great leader, Netaji.

The second conference in Singapore too was presided over by Rash Behari Bose. The presence of Netaji, the first he attended in East Asia, made the conference singularly unique. Towards the close of his (last) presidential address, Rash Behari Bose announced his resignation as president of the Indian Independence League in favour of Netaji Subhas Chandra Bose. Henceforth, he said, Subhas Chandra Bose would be the leader of the Indians in East Asia and would be their president. Subhas, he said, was the symbol of all that was best, the noblest, the most daring and the most dynamic in the youth of India and added that be brought Suhbhas from Tokyo as a present for the Indians in East Asia. The entire gathering was visibly moved at that moment – moved because of excitement of getting such a worthy present and the agony of parting with a noble and mature soul.

J.A. Thivy, the then chairman of the Malaya branch of the Indian Independence League, welcomed the president. He paid the new president the highest tributes which words could pay. The new president then addressed the meeting. The whole audience was spellbound and all listened to their great leader with careful attention.

Rash Behari Bose – The Unswerving Patriot

There is no parallel in our history for such an act as that of Rash Behari Bose in handing over power and position in such a magnificent style. The movement under the new president forms the second part of this book and before I close this part, I would like to give a brief account of the activities of Rash Behari Bose who became the supreme adviser to the president of the Indian Independence League in East Asia, Subhas Chandra Bose.

A born revolutionary and an ardent patriot, Rash Behari Bose was from his very early age wedded to the cult of the bomb and the revolver. He belonged to that category of the political revolutionaries of India who were convinced that the only way to destroy British imperialism founded on force was the use of force against it and that force alone would destroy it. Thus convinced, he launched his revolutionary activities in India even before the First World War – much before the Indian National Congress obtained the support and guidance of Mahatma Gandhi. The British wanted to arrest Rash Behari Bose. They pursued him from place to place and ultimately, he had to leave his motherland to save his life. He escaped to Japan. There, too, he was not left in peace. The octopus Britain tried to catch him from there. They offered a reward of Rs. 12,000 on his head and the Japanese government was requested to apprehend him for the British. Had it not been for the power of Toyama, the leader of the Black Dragon Society, Japan would have given away Rash Behari Bose.

The man who stayed the hands of Japan and set aside his arrest did it purely out of love and regard for the young Indian revolutionary. He helped him to settle down in that country, and Rash Behari Bose was there in Japan when the war broke out in the East.

Rash Behari Bose became a Japanese subject, got married to a wealthy Japanese and lived there. All those years of his stay in Japan, he used to write in English as well as in Japanese such articles of interest to Japan and India that he became popular in Japan. His desire to liberate India remained ever fresh in his mind. Though a Japanese subject by law, he remained an Indian at heart to his very last. His wife and children could speak and write Bengali as well as Hindustani. He wrote several books on India, her people, her past as well as the future to be. These were well received in that country.

Rash Behari Bose was determined that he would never return to India until she was free. The Indian Independence League in East Asia was the fruit of his labour. His assuming the leadership of the Indians in East Asia was purely and solely to serve the cause of India, which he always held dearer to him than his life. There was none in East Asia who could lead the movement as well as he did. When he found one who could do it better, he readily surrendered this great position to him and accepted his leadership with great pleasure.

Rash Behari Bose was not a domineering leader and was absolutely devoid of pride and desire for show of power – those common curses we find in many a leader. He never craved for power for its own sake. As a leader he was not without faults. But they were not of any serious type. He judged people wrongly. The most outstanding example was his poor judgement of people who associated with him. He simply trusted them and loved them even though some of them were the worst of crooks. He loved them in spite of their faults and trusted them. He was so tolerant and polite that to some people he seemed weak, which he was not. Behind his gentleness and politeness was a firmness and determination which only a revolutionary could command. He was ever ready to admit his faults and was ready to reason at all times.

Though advanced in years, Rash Behari Bose was a keen sportsman. He arranged for a football match between the Indians and an international team consisting of Japanese, Thais and Chinese. He called some of us to his office on the day previous to the match and simply selected eleven of us for the game. He even specified the positions in which we were to play. The match was played in the Bangkok stadium and in the presence of a very large gathering. Many high ranking officers of the Thai and Japanese forces and the foreign minister of Thailand were present. Lt. Ratan Singh of the Indian National Army and myself were the youngest of the players on the Indian side. We played and the match was a draw with each side scoring twice. The foreign minister of Thailand gave us all individual presents – silver tie pins. He was our host at a banquet that evening.

Despite such qualities, Rash Behari Bose apparently failed to lead the Indians in East Asia in the freedom fight. The most important reason for this failure was the distrust and suspicion of the Indians in his leadership. They thought him to be a Japanese agent. This was mostly caused by some of those Indians who came with him from Japan and moved closely with him. They shamelessly abused the trust and confidence he had in them. These men did all they could to poison Indian minds against him and get popularity for them. Some of those people came purely for enjoyment and not to work for India's freedom. Their morals were weak. Many people thought that the man who entrusted such people with responsibility might well be sharing their motives as well.

There were some honest and sincere workers among those who came with Rash Beharl Bose from Japan. D.S. Deshpandey, Ramsingh Rawel, J.K. Parikh and V. Supanaiker were prominent among them. While the headquarters of the League was at Bangkok, none dared to report to Rash Behari Bose about the viles and follies of any of the members of the Tokyo group; they were known as such then. But, when he was informed of such things later in Singapore, he made inquiries about those "silly scoundrels" and simply cast them away from the positions of importance in which they were placed. That was the highest punishment he could give.

The impression of doubt and suspicion that Rash Behari Bose was a Japanese agent remained only as long as he headed the movement. With his resignation as president of the independence movement, Indians understood him better. They soon learned that the man whom they feared or suspected to be a Japanese agent was one of the greatest Indian patriots and was solely and purely a great agent of Indian nationalism, patriotism and honour.

Still, many did him injustice in earlier days. Quite a large number of his countrymen misjudged him. They spread rumours against him and slandered him. They called him a Japanese spy. General Mohan Singh called him 'Oomachand' (traitor). They simply did not know him and never had the patience to find out the truth about him.

Some of the Indians, who lost faith in Rash Behari Bose because of his long stay in Japan, were themselves away from India for decades; might have been in some other country. They imagined in their thoughtless innocence that Rash Behari Bose would not be true and loyal to India because of his long stay in Japan and his association with the people of that country. They did not realise then that they themselves despite being outside India for several years claimed to love India just as much or more than those who had all along been there in India.

Absence, it is said, makes the heart grow fonder. This was so in the case of Rash Behari Bose. His one passion throughout his long stay in Japan was his motherland.

Whoever misjudged him at first realised afterwards, as they came in closer contact with him, that he was one of the greatest Indian patriots. No Indian loved his motherland more than Rash Behari Bose did. One of the most heartrending passages in his speech was "if my opponents call me a puppet, let them do so, but let me assure them that they are sinning against an old man whose only end and aim in life is to see his country free.............................. I shall retire into seclusion in some nook or corner of our beautiful motherland."

Most lives harbour some tragic note or the other and the life of Rash Behari Bose was no exception. His one great object was to see India free. He had to depart before he could see India free. For thirty years he lived a life of exile nurturing this ambition. Year in and year out he might have longed, yearned and pained to go back to an India that was free, to stand on that sacred soil of his birth, to live there and to die there. "I have lived my life," he used to say. "The only thing left for me is to enjoy the freedom of India." Once that was accomplished he was willing and ready to retire into some peaceful hamlet in the slopes of the Himalayas or on the banks of the Ganges and be a mere onlooker. "We shall look on to see how India freed would look like in her glory." That was denied to him.

Soon after the second conference in Singapore, Rash Behri Bose went back to Tokyo. He was weak and ailing and his doctors and friends advised him to take rest in some cool place. Before his departure, he called us all and talked to us for a long time. He told me that he would return to Singapore and go to Burma as soon as he got back his health. We had a group photo. We were very much moved at his leaving and we were sorry for his health and sorry for his departure.

He wrote to us in the League headquarters. He expressed great concern about the movement and said that as soon as he was fit for work, he would join us for active service in the struggle for the freedom of India. He was eager to know about the health and particulars of all those whom he knew and sent them his love.

On 22 January 1945, news came from Tokyo that Rash Behari Bose passed away. The Japanese news agency 'Domei' gave the following news with a brief note of his great life. "Rash Behari Bose, supreme adviser to the provisional government of Free India, well known Indian patriot and father of the Indian Independence League movement in East Asia, died of chronic ailment at his home in Tokyo at 2.00 a.m. on 21 January 1945."

In his last hours, Rash Behari Bose might have had the vision of his beloved India not as a land of the conquered, the sick and the palsied, of the oppressed and the starving, but as a land of glory, a land that is free, the home of men walking erect with heads upright, happy and contended and living the good life that providence has bestowed upon man. His vision came true? May his spirit guide the freedom loving people of Hindustan and join them in "The Land of the Free."

The League headquarters at Singapore arranged a condolence meeting on 28 January 1945, seven days after his demise. I was on that day on my way to Singapore from Bangkok. The meeting, I was told, was not well attended but the speakers, and particularly K. Raghavan paid very high tributes to the departed leader.

I have said what I wanted to say about Rash Behari Bose. I have nothing more to say about him here and I shall move on to the latter part of our struggle under the great and dynamic leader Netaji Subhas Chandra Bose.

JAI HIND

PART 2

An East Asia Co-Prosperity Dream

I

New President Netaji Subhas Chandra Bose Leads Indians in East Asia

"British rule is the darkest crime in the world; on the ashes of British imperialism, born of greed and robbery, will grow a happy and united India"

—Netaji

Even as Mahatma Gandhi and Pandit Jawaharlal Nehru were the top leaders of the Indian National Congress and the Indian people, Netaji Subhas Chandra Bose was an equally great leader of the Indian National Congress and the Indian people. He was the 52nd president of the Indian National Congress and was elected again as the 53rd president even against the expressed opposition of Mahatma Gandhi. However, he resigned the presidentship and founded the 'Forward Block' and was the president of it.

His disappearance from India, early in 1940, was a great misfortune that caused grief and concern to millions of Indians within and outside the country. In temples, mosques and churches they prayed for him, his health and safe return. To the British government and her police in India the escape from prison of their greatest opponent in

India was a stunning blow. Their all-out efforts and frantic search for his recapture were of no use. He reached his destination safe and sound. He appeared in Berlin where he was warmly welcomed and received by Hitler and the high officials of Nazy Germany.

Netaji joined Hitler at a time when Britain was almost at the mercy of the Fuehrer. His joining Hitler at such a time made Winston Churchill, the prime minister of Britain, boil with rage and curse him. The Germans were happy and even proud in getting Netaji on their side; his broadcasts over the Berlin radio and his appeals to the Indian soldiers had a very disastrous effect on the British war efforts. These served the Germans what could only have been accomplished with many thousand bombers and much more soldiers. Tens of thousands of Indian soldiers whom the British took to Africa to fight for them refused to fight the Germans and many laid down their arms at the bid of Netaji. This infuriated the British very much, but they were helpless and were unable to do anything to stop him.

In Germany, Netaji organised an Indian National Army from the volunteers out of the Indian prisoners of war there at that time. The Germans gave assistance and all possible facilities for training and equipping that army with most up-to-date arms and ammunition. The flag used by that army was the Indian national flag with a leaping tiger on it in place of the spinning wheel. This army, several thousand strong, was eagerly waiting to fight for the liberation of India at the call of Netaji.

Rash Beharl Bose, once spoke to Netaji from Bangkok on the transcontinental telephone. He invited Netaji to take over the leadership of the Indian Independence

League in East Asia. Netaji was at that time hoping to enter India with his army from the North West, with the aid and support of the German armed forces. And so he told Rash Behari Bose accordingly, and assured him that they would meet in India, meaning that Rash Behari might enter India from the East with the Indian National Army.

Fortunately or unfortunately, Netaji's hopes faded after the Germans instead of winning the war started to withdraw in defeat and his plan of entering India from the North West with his army of liberation was thus lost for ever. The Japanese were at that time fighting a winning war. Netaji came away to the East to lead the battle from there. He came to Japan in a German submarine, which took him from the Island of Crete to some secret base in Japan, from where he reached Tokyo.

As mentioned earlier, Rash Behari Bose was in Tokyo to receive his Illustrious brother, to inform him all about the movement and also to show him around. The Japanese government appointed two high ranking Japanese officials to assist Netaji; General Senda who was for long been in Calcutta and knew Netaji personally and Col Yamamotto who was attached to the Japanese embassy in Berlin and who came along with Netaji in the same under-sea craft.

Two days after the arrival of his distinguished guest in Tokyo, Premier General Tojo declared in a special statement that his government was prepared to help India win her freedom. It was his third public utterance since he started the Greater East Asia War for the East Asia Co-prosperity Sphere. Netaji called on him and other great leaders of Japan. Everywhere he was received with honour and warmth. He was also received by the Emperor of

Japan and was assured of all possible help in the fight for the liberation of India.

Netaji addressed the press on 19 June 1943 and also on the two subsequent days. Of course, these were the usual formalities, which Rash Behari Bose too had to undertake before assuming leadership. But there was a difference. Netaji Subhas Chandra Bose was an honoured guest of the Japanese while Rash Behari Bose was an old guest who ceased to be a guest and became a member of their family. Soon afterwards, Netajl and his party left for Singapore.

Accompanied by Gen Senda and Col Yamamotto, Rash Behari Bose and Abad Hassan, his private secretary, Netaji arrived in Singapore on 2 July 1943. A well furnished bungalow, new automobiles, picked INA and Gurkha body guards were all there, arranged in advance for the would-be president of the Indian Independence League, East Asia. It was noteworthy that Rash Behari Bose had no body guards. The formal reception and handing over of chair have all been described earlier.

The new president had a very busy and crowded programme. For the next few days, he used to attend his office at the League head quarters during the mornings. On 5 July 1943, the new leader held a review of the Indian National Army. All the officers and men of the Army took part in that function. Lt. Col N.Z. Khiani, commanded the Army. Ltd. Col Bhonsle and Captain Sheigal, the director and secretary, respectively, of the Military Bureau, were also prominently there. This impressive ceremony held in the Padang in front of the Singapore municipal buildings, was witnessed by a large number of Indians and other people. The whole function was repeated the next day in honour of General H. Tojo, the Premier of Japan. The General stood on the dais by the side of Netaji and saluted along with him the Indian National Army, which marched in columns before them. Tojo looked too small by the side of the towering Netaji.

I once read a book 'Malaya Upside Down' by a historian who said that he was filling the gap of Malaya's history. Out of his eagerness and enthusiasm to court the favour of his British masters, he wrote in that book that Subhas Chandra Bose marched in front of Tojo. Netaji was a much more formidable foe of British imperialism than Tojo and the "great historian" might have conceived that by insulting Netaji he would please his masters. The whole march past of the INA and the two leaders standing on the dais, side by side saluting the Army were witnessed by more than a hundred thousand people, including Malays, Chinese, Japanese, Eurasians and Indians and photographs of the same appeared in all the leading newspapers of the day.

Those keen on ascertaining the truth would do well to ask someone with good memory and who was there on that day or search for a copy of the day's newspaper. It is not difficult to do either. To the pro-British elements – there were many among the local population – the sight of Netaji standing on the dais, the smart and powerful army and its march past must have been a cause of severe headache.

Under the auspices of the Indian Independence League, a public meeting was held in the Padang on 9 July 1943. Never before was such a meeting held in Singapore in all its history. That meeting was unique in two respects. It was the first time that such a huge gathering of men of all nationalities assembled in Singapore. Secondly, the whole gathering stood in a heavy downpour for more than an hour; the speaker and the audience exposed to the heavy rain. Netaji spoke for more than two hours. The resolute stand of the audience amply convinced Netaji of the undaunted enthusiasm and determination of the Indians to do all in their power for the furtherance of the freedom movement as also their trust in his leadership.

In his fiery speech, he said that he had announced to the world about the formation of the Indian National Army and that he would soon start a historic march to Delhi. He added amidst cheers that 'Chhalo Delhi' would be the slogan for that march to India. Till the British are routed and the INA held its parade in the Red Fort in Delhi the Army would not rest for a moment, he said. In order to carry out the task before them, he offered toil, forced marches, hunger and death to those who were to follow him. The power, he said, which could not prevent his going out would never be able to stop his entry into India.

On 12 July 1943, Netaji addressed a meeting of the Indian women who gathered in large numbers. The newspapers said of it as the women's rally. The leader announced the formation of the Rani of Jhansi Regiment. The women and girls were thrilled at the announcement. Many offered to join the regiment.

All the speeches and statements of Netaji Subhas Chandra Bose have appeared in book form and I am not repeating them here again.

The following day, Netaji issued a circular giving particulars of the reorganised League headquarters. New departments were created and secretaries and officers were appointed for the work. Things began to improve and progress rapidly. The dynamic leadership of Netaji instilled courage and enthusiasm in all the workers of the organisation. There was wide awakening among the Indian women in East Asia and in response to his call large numbers of them joined the Rani of Jhansi Regiment and the Red Cross organisation.

Military training for civilians started and recruits rushed in to be enlisted and trained. In 1942, before the crisis in the Army, volunteers were called for military training. They came in large numbers. But, owing to the unhelpful attitude of the Japanese, the scheme had to be dropped. And, now, the very same Japanese were earnestly co-operating to open new camps for military training. Camps were opened in four places in Malaya alone and training started in earnest. An officer's training school (OTS) was also opened in Singapore to train Subalterns for the INA from among the NCOs and sepoys of the Army as well as from among civilians.

Indians, both rich and poor, contributed money and materials for the movement. They started assuming an optimistic view regarding the entire activities of the organisation and the impending battle for freedom. Large number of young men hurried to enlist for military training, but most of them had to wait as the camps were full.

The Japanese presented Netaji with an aero plane. The plane was named 'Netaji's Plane' and was used for his own tours. It was piloted by a Japanese. He first used that plane for his first trip to Bangkok. The Indians in Bangkok welcomed their great leader heartily and with great joy and enthusiasm. He was the guest of the Thai government and was honoured and treated like a head of government. Netaji spent most of his time there meeting prominent Indians who called at his residence one after another and offered large sums of money and materials for the movement. Netaji met the prime minister of Thailand and also other senior ministers. He addressed several public meetings, where also the Indians offered money and materials. After a week's stay in Bangkok, Netaji returned to Singapore.

His return to the headquarters was eagerly awaited and the news of his arrival brought several high ranking officers of the INA and some prominent Indians to the headquarters to see him. He came to the office as usual, at 9.00 a.m. that day.

I was the first to be called by Netaji and I was glad and somewhat elated in the honour. He received me smiling his best. After a minute or so of silence, he asked me about the overseas department's activities. The answers I gave were quite satisfactory to him. My first interview with Netaji lasted more than twenty minutes.

Coming out from his room, his private secretary Hassan asked me about the interview. I told him as to what happened; I was unable to understand the reason for the urgency of calling me, but Hassan was able to explain. At Bangkok, a German lady called on Netaji and also she offered her services to the Rani of Jhansi regiment. And Netaji wanted to see me for that reason. That German lady happened to be a good friend of mine – a chemistry graduate from Berlin and an artist of fame in Bangkok.

The new president started reorganisation of the Indian Independence League headquarters early in August 1943. Fourteen departments were organised, which included the general secretariat, military, finance, training, recruitment, education and culture, supplies, women's issues, reconstruction, press, publicity and propaganda, health and social welfare, overseas affairs and the housing departments.

Each of the civil departments was put under the control and charge of a secretary. In accordance with the reorganisation of the headquarters, instructions were issued to all the League branches in East Asia to carry out similar reorganisation in their offices and give effect to them immediately.

Netaji assumed supreme command of the INA (Azab Hind Fauj) on 8 August 1943, and the director of the Military Bureau became the chief of staff of the Indian National Army. Thus unification of command and better co-ordination have been effected and the whole of the League organisation was put on firm war-footing. One of the main features of the reorganisation was better coordination between the various departments of the League and the INA as well as the Japanese authorities.

The general secretariat was vastly expanded in order to cope with the volume of work that had piled up. Co-ordination between the different departments, the Indian National Army and the Japanese authorities has been well-established and the work proceeded smoothly.

Many changes have been given effect to in the Indian National Army since Netaji took over the supreme command. This boosted the morale of the Army and brought in contentment among the troops whose pay and rations were increased under orders of Netaji. Every effort was made to improve the conditions of the Army and to provide them with supplementary articles for diet in order to make them fully fit for the battle ahead. It became very necessary to collect more money and materials for the use of the Army and the organisation which maintained it.

The finance department was completely reorganised. Audit and accounts of the various departments and institutions started and the accounting system in each institute was regularised. Netaji made stirring appeals to Indians in East Asia for money and materials. The response to his appeal in almost all places had been instantaneous. Donations were received both in cash and in kind. Over 15 million dollars were collected in a short time. The average expenditure per month at that time was over two and half million dollars. But it was expected that it would incur a cost of five million dollars per month to train more men and to equip the Army fittingly.

Training in four centres has been firmly established and efforts were made to open some more. The instructors for training the volunteers were obtained from the Indian National Army through the co-operation of the military department. The Azad School organised a Japanese language course in addition to the training department. This was for training interpreters.

The training for civil volunteers, according to Netaji's instructions had been divided into three stages. In the first stage, the trainee had to spend a part of his leisure time for physical training and military drill and during this period he was not required to leave his home or give up his occupation. In the second stage, these volunteers were sent to actual training centres, when new courses or sessions started. And, in the third stage when the volunteers completed their initial course in training centres, they were absorbed into the Indian National Army.

The enthusiasm and spirit shown by the volunteers during and after their military training have been commendable. It was not possible to equip them to the extent desired but in spite of difficulties and hardships, the volunteers kept their high spirits during the strenuous training and were ever prepared to go to the forefront of the battle for which they waited anxiously. It may be mentioned that the tradesmen recruited for the Army, like washermen, tailors and barbers, insisted on being trained in the use of arms as soldiers for at least a certain period every day in addition to their professional task. They said that they were soldiers first and this illustrated the indomitable spirit of the volunteers of the INA.

The recruiting of the civil volunteers started in right earnest. They were medically examined and were sent to the different centres of training established in Malaya, Burma and other places. There were many overseas recruits.

The education and culture department was established to encourage and impart spiritual education and teach national subjects amongst the Indians in East Asia. Pamphlets for this purpose were published and sent to all the League branches.

The supply department rapidly grew into a powerful and dynamic distributive system. This department, under the able leadership of Haridayal Singh, Lab Singh and Jamnadas Mehta who all were leading business men of Malaya, arranged to procure and supply various articles required by the INA and the League headquarters. It also established supply depots at different places to meet the requirements of the various training camps and also the Indian National Army.

The women's department, which formed an integral part of the organisation, was headed by Captain Lakshmi of the Rani of Jhansi Regiment, named after the famous Rani of Jhansi who died fighting in the battlefield in the First War of Independence in 1857. The department organised a Red Cross unit. Thus, Indian women offered to serve in the INA, to bear arms to fight and nurse the wounded.

Women in India have at all times shared the joys and sorrows with men and it was a great pleasure to observe the same spirit prevailing outside India also.

The reconstruction department was established to train young and intelligent cadets in civil administration work in order that they might be used in occupied territories in India. Devastation during the war was inevitable and it was, therefore, necessary to have a nucleus of trained civil administrators to establish civil administration in occupied territory. The subjects they were taught were those closely concerned with civil administration such as maintenance of law and order, production, supply and distribution of food, prevention of epidemics, restoration of public utility services etc.

The publicity, press and propaganda department under the able and experienced secretaries S.A. Iyer and M. Sivaram did its work well. It was publishing altogether four daily and two weekly newspapers and was controlling and directing the Indian section of broadcasting in Singapore, Bangkok, Saigon, Rangoon and Tokyo. Following a conference held in Bangkok in connection with broadcasting, various changes were effected in the programme of work with a view to increasing its efficiency.

The health and social welfare department was organised in order to supervise health and social welfare programmes for both the civil volunteers as well as the civil population. Very little progress was possible due to the existing conditions and there was shortage of qualified men for such work.

The housing department was established to look after the lodging of the workers of the League headquarters and also the accommodation of various delegates who came to attend conferences.

The overseas department coordinated the activities of the various branches of the Indian Independence League in the different territories of East Asia. It did very useful work in collecting information from the different branches of the League scattered over a large area – important pieces of information relating to the availability of men, materials and money in the localities where we had our branches. I was in charge of this new department from the beginning to the very end. I traveled throughout East Asia, on inspection tours of the League branches. There were some 212 branches of the League and the membership was about 300,000.

Netaji ordered that the entire officers other than military officers and all the staff and workers of the League headquarters should undergo military training under special instructors appointed for that purpose. They were also to learn Hindustani as well as the Japanese language. Training and learning started in earnest but somehow these soon came to a stop. The secretary general carefully kept silent about this and did not dare to inform Netaji about it.

In order to strengthen the movement further, Netaji decided to form the Provisional Government of Free India. The representatives of the Indian community in East Asia were all invited to Singapore. They came on or before 20 October 1943. They all, like all of us, awaited eagerly for the historic meeting, which was scheduled to be held the next morning.

II

Declaration of the Provisional Government of Azad Hind

On 21 October 1943, Indian delegates from all over East Asia assembled at the Cathay Hall in Singapore for a great occasion. At that meeting, amidst deafening applause and loud cheers, Netaji Subhas Chandra Bose announced the formation of the Provisional Government of Azad Hind.

After stating briefly the history and course of the long struggle for the freedom of India, Netaji said that with the Congress ministries in eight provinces in India from

1937–1939, Indians had given proof of their readiness and their capacity to administer their own affairs.

The stage was set for the final struggle for India's liberation. Netaji declared this on the eve of the Second World War.

"During the course of the war, Germany, with the help of her allies, has dealt shattering blows to our enemy in Europe while Nippon, with the help of her allies has inflicted a knockout blow to our enemy in East Asia. Favoured by a most happy combination of circumstances, the Indian people today have a wonderful opportunity for achieving the national emancipation."

"For the first time in history, Indians abroad have also been politically roused and stood united as one organisation. They were not only thinking and feeling in tune with their countrymen at home, but were also marching in step with them, along the path of freedom. In East Asia, in particular, over a million Indians stood as one solid Phalanx, inspired by the slogan of 'total mobilisation.' And in front of them stood the ranks of India's army of liberation with the slogan 'Onward to Delhi' on their lips."

"Having goaded the Indians to desperation by its hypocrisy and having driven them to starvation and death by plunder and loot, British rule in India has forfeited the goodwill of the Indian people altogether and is now living a precarious existence. It needs but a flame to destroy the last vestige of that unhappy rule. To light that flame is the task of India's Army of Liberation. Assured of the enthusiastic support of the civil population at home and also of a large section of Britain's Indian

Army, and backed by gallant and invincible allies abroad but relying in the first instance on its own strength, India's Army of Liberation was confident of fulfilling its historic role."

"Now that the dawn of freedom is at hand, it is the duty of the Indian people to set up a provisional government of their own and launch the last struggle under the banner of that government. But, with almost all Indian leaders in prison and the people at home totally disarmed, it was not possible to set up a provisional government within India or to launch an armed struggle under the aegis of that government. It was, therefore, the duty of the Indian Independence League in East Asia, supported by all patriotic Indians at home and abroad, to undertake the task of setting up a Provisional Government of Azad Hind (Free India) and of conducting the last fight for freedom, with the help of the Army of Liberation, ie, the Azad Hind Fauj or the Indian National Army, organised by the League."

"Having been constituted as the Provisional Government of Azad Hind by the Indian Independence League in East Asia, we enter upon our duties with full sense of the responsibility that has devolved on us. We pray that Providence may bless our work and our struggle for the emancipation of our motherland. And we hereby pledge our lives and the lives of our comrades in arms to the cause of her freedom, of her welfare, and her exaltation among the nations of the world."

"It will be the task of the Provisional Government to launch and conduct the struggle that will bring about the expulsion of the British and their allies from the soil of India. It will then be the task of the Provisional

Government to bring about the establishment of a permanent national government of Azad Hind, constituted in accordance with the will of the Indian people and enjoying their confidence. After the British and their allies are overthrown and until a permanent national government of Azad Hind is set up on Indian soil, the Provisional Government will administer the affairs of the country in trust for the Indian people."

"The provisional government is entitled to, and hereby claims, the allegiance of every Indian. It guarantees religious liberty, as well as equal rights and equal opportunities to all its citizens. It declares the firm resolve to pursue the happiness and prosperity of the whole nation and of all its parts, cherishing all the children of the nation equally and transcending all the differences cunningly fostered by an alien government in the past."

"In the name of God, in the name of bygone generations who have welded the Indian people into one nation, and in the name of the dead heroes who have bequeathed to us a tradition of heroism and self sacrifice, we call upon the Indian people to rally round our banner and to strike for India's freedom. We call upon them to launch the final struggle against the British and all their allies in India and to execute that struggle with valour and perseverance and with full faith in the final victory when the enemy is expelled from India's soil and the Indian people are once again a free nation."

The declaration was signed on behalf of the Provisional Government of Azad Hind by Subhas Chandra Bose, head of state, prime minister, minister for war and foreign affairs. It was also signed by three other ministers, Captain Lakshmi, S.A. Ayer and Lt. Col A.C. Chatterji and eight representatives of the Army, namely, Lt. Col Aziz Ahmed, Lt. Col M.S. Bhagat, Lt. Col J.K. Bhonsle, Lt. Col Gulzara Singh, Lt. Col M.Z. Khiani, Lt. Col A.D. Loganathan, Lt. Col Ehsan Qadir, Lt. Col Shah Nawaz, A.M. Sahay, secretary with ministerial rank and Rash Beharl Bose as supreme adviser. Six others signed the declaration as advisers and A.N. Sarkar signed as legal adviser. Captain Lakshmi was the minister for women, S.A. Ayer was the minister for publicity and propaganda and Lt. Col A.C. Chatterji was the minister for finance.

Netaji was overwhelmed with emotion and was sobbing and in tears when he read out the last paragraph of the declaration. In the name of God........, and this moved the entire audience who were spell-bound and were in suspense for a while.

The declaration was a great step forward in the battle for freedom and the entire Indian population in East Asia was happy and rejoiced over it. Even the poor Indian labourers were happy and elated and most of them thought that they were already a free people. The delegates who came from the different regions returned proud and happy.

III

The Free India Government

"After passing through an ordeal of oppression, deaths, misery and starvation since August 1942, India had made great advances in its fight for freedom,"

—Jawaharlal Nehru.

When he said these words, Pandit Nehru might have had in his mind all about the activities of the Provisional Government of Free India. The recognition of that government by eight great powers added prestige to it. The formal declaration of war by that government on Britain and America surely added momentum to the determination of the Indians to fight a total war for total victory. Nehru might even have changed his whole attitude towards the war in the East in regard to his earlier assertion: "Even if Subhas Chandra Bose comes at the head of a Japanese army, India will fight to the last."

The entire organisation of the Indian independence movement throbbed with vitality and vigour and the INA declared its readiness to begin the march to Delhi. Hurried preparations were made to shift the headquarters of the Provisional Government of Azad Hind and that of the Indian Independence League from Singapore to Rangoon, where it would be nearer to the Indian boarder, the theatre of war.

Most of the secretaries and staff of the headquarters in Singapore remained there while a few left for Rangoon. The Singapore headquarters was named the rear headquarters. On 7 January 1944, the headquarters started to function at Rangoon.

Some more ministers were appointed and among them N. Raghavan was given the portfolio of finance. Officers of the INA were promoted and all the Colonels became Major Generals. Junior officers, too, received promotions similar to the seniors. S.A. Ayer, who was minister of publicity and propaganda was appointed vice president of the Indian Independence League in East Asia. He was also the secretary to the provisional government.

The Andaman and Nicobar Islands were occupied by the Japanese long before. They gave these islands to the Provisional Government of Azad Hind. Netaji Subhas Chandra Bose visited the island in connection with the taking over of its administration. The Indians there rejoiced and they assembled near Port Blair to listen to their leader who spoke to them for more than two hours. There, for the first time, Netaji stood on free Indian soil where the tricolour flag of India fluttered high on roof-tops of all the homes and offices. Maj General A.D. Loganathan with his staff took over the administration of the islands as the first high commissioner of the islands, the first to be appointed by the Provisional Government of Azad Hind.

In India, the widespread famine and deaths due to starvation and hunger were causes for deep concern to Netaji. He wanted to do his best to save the people from that British made famine in his motherland. He offered a hundred thousand tons of rice from Burma as a free gift to India. This sincere offer was made over the radio. He earnestly requested the Government of India to send the required ships to carry the rice from Rangoon to India and he guaranteed the safe return of all the vessels sent for that purpose. The proud and ever-haughty British government in India did not pay any heed to this humanitarian offer: What did it matter to the British if Indians died in thousands every hour due to starvation and hunger?

The shortage of qualified doctors for service with the Indian National Army was very much felt, though most of the Indians qualified for such service joined the Army at the call of Netaji. Dr. R.K. Prasad, who joined the INA from Kuala Lumpur donated all his money and medicines (more valuable than gold at the time) worth more than two hundred thousand dollars to the INA and joined it as Maj Prasad. He served it faithfully to the last. Later he became well known in India too due to his stand against the shooting of the INA prisoners at the Calcutta camp.

The new finance minister of the Provisional Government of Azad Hind was, as already mentioned, the most popular Indian leader of Malaya and he was able to collect large sums of money and materials as donations for the movement from all parts of Malaya. He campaigned for that and addressed meetings in the various cities of Malaya.

The Rani of Jhansi camp was a place of great activity for young Indian women and girls from the different regions of East Asia. They received good training in the art of war as well as in nursing. Col Lakshmi, who commanded the unit, was an able organiser and she did the work entrusted to her very well. She had to go to Rangoon due to the transfer of the headquarters and Captain (Mrs.) Thevar was appointed to command the unit.

The Officers Training School in Singapore, or the OTS, as it was known, trained a large number of enthusiastic Indian youth in modern warfare. They underwent very tough training and were considered very good officers, even though their period of training was only six months. Some of the cadets who joined the school from overseas were sons of very rich Indians.

Netaji established his office in Rangoon from where he directed and controlled the movement in East Asia. The provisional government soon started publication of its gazette, copies of which were sent to all the 212 league branches in East Asia through the overseas department of the Indian Independence League rear headquarters in Singapore.

The official gazette had the emblem of the leaping tiger on its facing page and contained mostly government orders, including promotions of senior officers and their transfers from different regions, as also orders from Netaj as head of state and supreme commander of the INA. The gazette was published from Rangoon and usually signed by S.A. Iyer, who was the secretary to the Provisional Government of Azad Hind.

The Indians in Burma were not lagging in their efforts in the furtherance of the movement and the impending war of liberation. They offered huge amounts of money and materials and thousands of able bodied young Indians joined the Army. The Indians in Burma once donated Netaji's weight in gold as a birthday gift to their great leader – about 180 lbs of gold.

More than 12,000 officers and men of the Indian National Army from Malaya reached Burma as advance units of the Army to take part in their march to Delhi.

The Japanese at that time were not in favour of a big offensive against India due to certain setbacks they had in the Pacific regions, particularly in the Philippines. The American B-29s were creating havoc to the Japanese everywhere and the threatened invasion of Japan forced them to withdraw a good number of their handpicked officers to their homeland. But the Japanese were a very tough and tenacious people and they were determined to go ahead with the war. They used to say that Japan was prepared to fight the war for a hundred years; of course they knew little of the atom bombs when they said so.

The War of Liberation

Due to the Allied offensive in the Hukwang Valley and the threatened push down the Chindwin River the Japanese had to make all out efforts to defend and to hurl the allies backwards. Even then, the Japanese plan was to take Imphal and then let the INA go into action. Netajl Subhas Chandra Bose was not in favour of such moves by the Japanese and insisted on the INA taking part in the Arakan and Manipur campaigns.

On 4 February 1944, the Indian National Army went into action. And, on 18 March, they crossed the Indo-Burma border. It was big news for Indians everywhere. They were happy and rejoiced at it. Soon the INA detachments along with the Japanese detachments surrounded Imphal after occupying Moral, Kohima and other villages. The lack of air support and the disruption of the supply lines owing to the heavy monsoon forced our troops to withdraw.

But, in this first clash between the Indian National Army and the British troops, the Indian patriots gave a remarkably good account of themselves and proved that, given a chance, they could defeat and drive the British out of India. The courage, the fighting spirit and tenacity exhibited by the civil recruits, mostly erstwhile clerks and coolies from South India who joined the Indian National Army in Malaya and Burma, exploded once for all the martial-non-martial race theory of the British. The instances of sublime heroism and devotion evinced by the Indian National Army were numerous and remarkable and deserved universal praise.

Short of food, short of clothing, short of ammunition and even ill-equipped for a modern war, these brave soldiers fought and drove back one of the best equipped armies of the world. The men of the INA sometimes had to live on grass and yam leaves in the tropical villages and jungles on the Indo-Burma border; the Arakans, Palel and Imphal sectors. These hills and valleys have become sanctified by the blood of our beloved brothers who sacrificed their lives for our independence. Let us be proud of them; let us not forget them; let us remember them forever. Let the very air of those regions carry forever the echo of their shouts 'Inquilab Zindabad' and 'Azad Hind Zindabad.' They all died for the sake of India and our liberty. Their spirits ever remain high.

The second campaign of the INA, early in 1945, was a defensive one and was undertaken mainly for two reasons. First, the loss of Burma would hamper our movement. And, second, the Japanese deserved our help and support at that time. They fought by our side and we were benefited by their victories. Hence it would have been gross ingratitude on our part if we chose to remain as passive onlookers when the Japanese were in doldrums.

During this campaign, there were acts of treachery on the part of some of our officers; the worst being that of Major Madan, Major Riaz, Major Gulam Sawar and Major Dey. They were staff officers of the Indian National Army 2nd Division who defected to the enemy side. But they were only a few. Officers like Col Shaha Navaz, Col Prem Sahagal, Lt. Col Gurumit Singh, and Lt. Col Mehar

Das and many other junior officers and men stood and fought against numerically superior forces and fought heroically. The INA held its position and destroyed or wiped out two attempts of the enemy to cross the Irawady River. In the end, it was the Japanese sector which gave way to the enemy and the INA was forced to withdraw.

When Meyktila fell and the British 14th Army's progress was too fast for the Japanese to halt, they decided to evacuate Rangoon and thereby leave Burma. A force of about six thousand men and officers of the INA, it was decided by the supreme commander of our Army, was to remain in Rangoon. Maj Gen Bhonsle, the chief of staff, was to surrender Rangoon to the enemy but he pleaded for excuse and managed to get away in good time. He was a poor soldier. Maj Gen A.D. Loganathan volunteered to take the command of the INA and Netaji gladly accepted his offer. This old man was a far better soldier than the chief who flew away to Bangkok.

Netaji Subhas Chandra Bose and his government left Rangoon on 24 April 1945 for Bangkok. Netaji with S.A. Ayer and his personal aides and guards were the last to leave Rangoon. The Japanese government and their commander-in-chief left Burma on the previous day, ie, 23 April 1945. Netaji had to walk most of the way through hills and valleys, through thick forest heavily infested with wild animals and inhabited by barbaric tribes. Undaunted, he marched and reached Bangkok from where he flew to Singapore.

The officers of the INA and its men were entrusted with the most difficult task of protecting the lives and property of the Indians in Rangoon. Under the able leadership of that brave old man, Gen A.D. Loganathan, they did their job well and received praise from the enemy for that. The British found it difficult to maintain law and order without the help of the INA.

They took control of the city of Rangoon and there was not a single case of loot or dacoity during the time the INA controlled the city. Later reports showed that the Indian Independence League branches in Burma did very good service to the Indian community thereby preventing possible attacks on the lives and property of Indians in Burma.

The above events may well stand out in contrast to the notorious withdrawal of the British from Burma when they were unable to hold their own against the Japanese attack in 1942. That withdrawal was unique in history for the wanton destruction of lives and property of innocent civilians. It was worse than any scorched earth policy. The British asked the Indians to get ready for evacuation to India by sea and assured them that there were enough steamers ready. There were in all more than three hundred thousand people ready and willing to go to India. How could the British find transport for all of them? They transported a few thousand of them. The rest were ordered to march to India on foot from Rangoon. Those Indians, majority of whom were labourers.....men, women and children......with their household utensils, their cattle, their dogs and even cats, began the march. They marched for more than a hundred miles. Owing to lack of food and water they soon were exhausted and worn out and with their precious cargo they fell on the road like withered leaves. Some were ill, some were resting, others were sleeping on the highway along the way for a hundred miles. The British army withdrew at that time. They were in panic and with their heavy and medium tanks and armoured cars, equipment and arms, the army withdrew along the same road the Indians were lying. And these men were run over by the fast moving convoys of the British, grinding to death almost all of those three hundred thousand Indians. The tough Japanese soldiers found it a hard job to remove and bury the dead and decayed bodies of a hundred thousand Indians scattered over the road for a hundred miles or more. Has there ever been such an act of cruelty elsewhere among civilised people?

The part of the INA left at Rangoon surrendered to the British on 25 April 1945. Maj Gen Loganathan, on behalf of the INA and Brigadier Laudor of the 36th Indian Infantry on behalf of the British took part in that function. The British adopted their typical policy of hypocrisy in their treatment of the surrendered personnel. The British brigadier told the INA general that the INA personnel would be allowed to go back to India and on his request Gen Loganathan agreed to remove the INA ranks of his men and officers. And those who were previously in the British army were required to put on their old uniforms and ranks. The brigadier also assured that the INA personnel would not be put to fatigue except in company with the Indian troops and that they would be allowed to remain in their own camps under their own control.

But, once they completed the disarming of the INA, the same brigadier ordered them to march to the Rangoon central prison and his attitude to them soon changed. Those men were forced to do hard labour, cleaning and sweeping the roads, under British guards. Fortunately they were not ordered to bury the dead bodies on the roads, there were none. The INA officers were kept in prison and were closely guarded.

Netaji Returns to Singapore

Netaji established his headquarters once again in Singapore. He knew, as others also, that the days of the Japanese victory were over and that the Anglo-Americans would reach Malaya and the Japanese would have to withdraw or surrender. But none of us talked about such matters even among our friends. It was no more due to fear of Japanese reprisals as anti-Japanese but because we never wished to think of a British victory.

The Japanese started digging tunnels and trenches everywhere. They built one right under the hill on which I was residing at that time. I was told that the building was the official residence of the PWD chief engineer, Singapore in days before the war. The Japanese made a three-way tunnel below that hill, with spacious office rooms which could accommodate about four hundred of their men. They told me so. The Japanese used to say that they were preparing to fight a long war; might be for a hundred years. Many people even believed this.

Netaji Subhas Chandra Bose once suggested that the headquarters might be shifted to up-country Malaya, were the offices were to be scattered in different localities to avoid complete destruction by enemy bombs. Bombing of Singapore and Malaya at that time increased in intensity and number. We had individual trenches near our offices as well as our residences. Some of us never went to these trenches even during the heaviest of air raids as we learned that Netaji never went to any shelter during air raids. Once when he was about to land from his plane in the Bangkok airfield, enemy planes came overhead and showered their bombs on that field. Netaji walked across the field calmly, went inside a room in one of the buildings and simply sat there. He refused to move into an underground shelter nearby. He believed in fate and was never afraid of his life.

The shifting of the offices did not materialise. Only the reconstruction department was shifted from Singapore. It was removed to Serarapan in Johore state. Activities of the League headquarters went on as usual. Those days we found the Japanese more polite than before and they behaved to us as real brothers-in-arms. Their arrogance seemed to have gone, gone for good.

When we were almost certain of the Japanese fall, some of us made plans to join the Malayan communists who were then fighting the Japanese from the jungles of Malaya. The communists made us believe that they would fight the British and drive them out of Malaya. We offered to join them and negotiations were carried on between their leaders and some of our senior army officers. Col Bishen Singh, officer commanding the OTS and Col Gurumit Singh, the well known hockey player of India were prominent in such negotiations. I too took some part in it. But, soon, we had to break with the reds and that for no fault of ours.

We lived through the period in suspense awaiting certain doom. On 21 July 1945, senior INA officers, ministers of the Provisional Government of Azad Hind, department heads and senior officers of the Indian Independence League headquarters and prominent Indians of Singapore were present at a solemn ceremony when Netaji unveiled a memorial erected near the seashore of Singapore in memory of the Indian soldiers who died in battle.

On 13 August 1945, British planes dropped leaflets in thousands, announcing the expressed wish of the Japanese to surrender, after the atom bombing of Heroshima and Nagasaki. The leaflets were picked up by all those who found them. The Japanese showed no sign of excitement at such picking up of enemy's pamphlets and notices. So we all knew that everything the enemy announced were going to happen.

On 16 August 1945, Netaji called senior officers of the INA and the League headquarters to his office and told us that he was going to Bangkok to settle the financial affairs of the League branch there. We had gold worth several lakhs and much money there and so we all thought that he was going for a necessary trip. He ordered Maj Gen M.Z. Khiani and two other Maj Generals to act on his behalf in his absence from Singapore. We thought that was only a temporary arrangement. He left by plane for Bangkok early morning that was what we learned.

We hoped Netaji would return soon to join us at the time of surrender and we used to go to the office with that hope and nothing else. There was much money at the League headquarters, which was distributed in thousands to the staff and workers. The British pamphlets dropped soon afterwards announced that they would not pay for the Japanese currency and so the monetary value of the Japanese dollar was just zero and nothing more.

On the evening of 17 August, I visited the INA camp at Selatar, Singapore in company of three friends. There we were held up for long in our friendly chats with all those dear ones from whom it was difficult to take leave. We returned very late in the night. Seeing lights in the headquarters offices we went there. To our grief we saw heaps of files and papers on fire. When asked the reason for burning those records, we were told that those were set fire at the orders of Netaji. I was very sorry. I lost all my personal papers along with rare office files and records which were all ashes by that time. There was a copy of the film 'Chalo Delhi' which too went up in flames.

At that time, there were signs of some trouble going on in the stores department between the superintendent of the store and labourers of the headquarters who numbered about six hundred. The superintendent was a friend of mine and a good fellow. He was a weak man and was in trouble with those who demanded him clothes.

He refused on the ground that he had no orders to give them the stores they demanded. I told him that since the files and records were in flames there was no need for him for any order to distribute the stores. Reluctantly he agreed to give clothes to all the labourers. There was still more left of clothing even after distribution and there was a huge store of provisions and various other things worth a fortune. Being late and finding no one else, we closed the stores and went to our quarters to sleep. Early next morning we learned that the whole stores were looted.

Before his departure to Bangkok and also at an early date Netaji sent word to the finance minister N. Raghavan at Penang to go over to Singapore. There was no reply from him and he never came to Singapore. If he were in

Singapore, we would have been better in many respects. But Raghavan had his own family and friends at Penang and he thought it better to look after their affairs in time of danger.

The refusal of Raghavan to come to Singapore at that time and the going away of Netaji to Tokyo were two very important factors which affected a few of us left at the headquarters very deeply and we shall never be able to justify their action in any way. Some others might have explanations for Raghavan's refusal to come to Singapore and of Netaji's going away to Tokyo or wherever he liked. Anyway, their actions sure have changed the course of my life.

Japanese News of the Plane Crash

On 19 August 1945, the Japanese news agency "Domei" gave the most sorrowful and heart breaking news from Tokyo, that Netaji Subhas Chandra Bose, head of state and the supreme commander of the Indian National Army, died in a Japanese hospital due to burns and injuries he received in a plane crash. The accident was reported to have taken place at Fukuoka, near Formosa on the day before.

Since the setting up of the Indian Independence League in East Asia we had lost numerous lives; we lost four eminent patriots when the Japanese plane carrying them to Tokyo crashed near Issae Bay of Japan; we lost more than ten thousand of our own brothers in the battle for freedom; we lost the father of the movement, Rash Behari Bose who died of illness in Tokyo and, now, our great Netaji's, the greatest soldier of India's battle for freedom. It was the saddest phase of all our misfortunes. It was an irreparable loss to our motherland.

Those who remained at the League headquarters, officers and men of the INA and the Indians in Singapore, held a condolence meeting in Singapore. They mourned his death.

Many spoke on the occasion: they spoke about his past, about his greatness, about his determination to fight for the freedom of his motherland and of the sad fate which took him away. Indians everywhere in East Asia held similar meetings in their localities and they all wept at his loss and prayed for his soul. He was our most beloved leader, the greatest soldier India ever had and was worthy of the highest honour and place among the greatest of all the leaders of India.

I did not participate in the condolence meetings though I was officially invited for the same, mainly for two reasons. First, I was informed by a good and trust worthy Japanese friend who at that time was working with the chief of the Japanese news service 'Domei' in Singapore, that Netaji's plane crash was a Japanese stunt to save him from the Anglo-Americans. Second, I did not like his leaving us and going away to Tokyo or anywhere at that time, to escape from the enemy. My conception of a good leader and of Netaji himself was not in agreement with his abandoning his men in the hour of peril or at the time of surrender or the worst. And, I hope, you will agree with me that the fate of the INA and all of us who remained there would have been a different one had he stayed with us. The British who could not even punish those officers of their own army who joined the INA and fought against them would not have dared to do any harm to Netaji Subhas Chandra Bose, the supreme commander of the Indian National Army and the idol of India. You can well imagine the great occasion, if he were with us on his return to India.

Netaji might have had own ideas. He was never involved in the so-called plane crash and he did not die in any plane crash. It is now almost 75 years since and so it is not at all possible to say whether he was alive or dead. Let us pray for his soul as we did for his safe return in 1940 when he vanished from India.

To those who do not agree with me and to those who believe the Japanese news of his death due to that plane accident I have this to tell. The Japanese government of those years of the Greater East Asia War of their Co-prosperity Sphere was not like the present one. Their emperor, their government, their armed forces, their people and many other things as we find of the Japanese were very much different from the present. It is well known and has been admitted by the Japanese themselves. They never wanted any of those leaders or heads of states who were with them in the war to fall into the enemy's hands. If they could, they would help it. They did what they thought would help them in their plan to save such allies. They tried to save Cheng En Po, who was buried by the Japanese news agencies. He was later arrested from Tokyo and was handed over to the Chinese government. Dr. Baw Maw and President Laural of the Philippines were missing in their respective countries, according to the Japanese. These two were also found and were arrested by the Americans. These are facts known and well publicised. So far there has been no trace of Netaji. He knew better than Laural or Baw Maw or Cheng En Po where to go and escape the enemy. We do not know where he went. He might have gone to China or possibly to India or wherever he liked.

The British re-occupation of Singapore and Malaya was almost a silent affair as there were no gun shots or bomb explosions, except once in Singapore when the silence was broken by the loud blasts of dynamite blowing up the INA monument erected in memory of the dead. The foremost task of the British forces on landing in Singapore, it seemed, was the destruction of that monument. Even to the British it was an act of the meanest and lowest type. None protested against that action and no one was rewarded or awarded 'Victoria Cross' for it.

Officers and men of the Indian National Army under the command of Maj Gen M.Z. Khiani surrendered their arms and ammunition like men of a civilised army. Yet, the British tried to humiliate and bully them whenever possible. On one occasion, a British major ordered Gen Khiani to strip off his uniform. He did so. The major further ordered him to remove all his under garments as well, to humiliate him. The General not only disobeyed that order but slapped the British on his face. Of course, Khiani was punished for that – he was put in prison for several days for his offence.

Indians in East Asia and particularly those of us left in Singapore felt miserable and sad. The news from New Delhi that the leaders of India were on our side and were getting ready to defend the Indian National Army and the Indian independence movement gave us some relief.

I used to visit the INA camp (the camp of the prisoners) in Singapore those days. During one of my visits, I was surprised to see Maj Gen A.C. Chatterji. He was the secretary general of the League headquarters before he became minister and went away to Rangoon. We were good friends and he was happy to see me in his prison camp. He praised me much and told me all about his story; the story of how he was brought to Singapore by the clever British spies. He and seven others were in Chinese territory on the borders of Indochina. The Chinese authorities were not prepared to offer them any plane trip. The British managed to bring them to Saigon on the assurance of a plane trip to Calcutta. Once they reached Saigon, the British suddenly changed their attitude; they arrested Chatterji and his seven followers. The British major in charge of the area thought it better to send the major general to the Selatar camp in Singapore and Chatterji was at last among many friends.

British security officers started interrogation of the senior officers of the INA and the members of the Indian Independence League headquarters in different places. One by one they picked up such Indians, drove them in their jeeps to their own camps and asked them questions after questions. It was difficult to answer some of their funny questions but answer they must. They took me for such interrogation seven times in a month. I answered many of their questions. Some I refused to answer and at last they left me in peace.

During that time, I had news from Borneo that the chairman of the Indian Independence League there, S.C.S. Chakravorthy and his son-in-law Dr. Gopal were badly beaten by the Australians who occupied that island and that they were put in prison for being officials of the Indian Independence League there. Dr. Gopal was my own cousin, with whom I had stayed in Kueking, Borneo. I was sorry for them and did not know what to do to save them. I wrote to the officer commanding the 8th Australian Army, which occupied Borneo, that those men whom they ill-treated and imprisoned were not responsible for the Indian Independence League in Borneo and that I was the one responsible for that organisation there. So, I requested their release and offered myself for the punishment if any. As expected, there was no reply. But I was glad to learn that they were soon released. But, again, several other Indians were arrested in Borneo, arrested on various criminal charges of collaboration with the Japanese.

The panel of Indian lawyers who visited Malaya came to Singapore at that time. I saw them at K.P. Kesava Menon's residence and acquainted them with the situation of Indians in Borneo. And, as suggested by them, I prepared a brief memorandum and took it personally to the Indian agent general in Singapore.

Kesava Menon was put in prison by the Japanese as they thought him anti-Japanese and was released by the British. He was of the opinion that the Japanese were not sincere and that Netaji was doomed to fail. He used to express these in talks with his friends which enraged the Japanese who imprisoned him.

The lawyers from India, K.P. Kesava Menon and some others, were present when I went to see the distinguished officer with my memorandum describing the grievances of the Indians in Borneo. My uniform and salute shouting 'Jai Hind' were quite unexpected to G.K. Chettur, the Indian agent general and it was seen on his face. After reading the memorandum, he asked me as to what he should do? I was very much surprised at the question. However, I told him politely to consult his government and do what it directed or ordered. This reply by me made Keshava Menon beckon me to his place. I went to him. He told me in Malayalam that I should not have spoken to the agent general as I did. I pointed out to him that after all that was what the officer could do and so there was no harm in my telling him so. Sapru junior was glad at my reply and he congratulated me for it. Later, I invited the panel of lawyers to my residence for tea with my friends at 329 Bukit Timah Road, Singapore. They came and we had hearty talk with the lawyers regarding our movement.

Reports regarding the suffering of the Indians in Borneo were submitted to Pandit Kunzru and the then president of the Indian National Congress Jawharlal Nehru, who was able to force the hand of the British government in India to appoint a lawyer to defend the Indians in Borneo who were imprisoned on criminal charges of collaboration with the Japanese. K.P. Kesava Menon was sent to Borneo as attorney. I was able to give him useful information. He did good work for the Indians in Borneo. He was able to get the acquittal of all the Indians except one against whom charges of murder were proved. By the time Menon returned from Borneo, I was waiting ready to secure passage to India. I was glad to hear from him the story of his success in Borneo and was happy to learn that he saved the Indians there from unnecessary and unwarranted ill-treatment by the British occupation forces. Before my departure to India, actually on the day previous to it, Menon was at home with me and my relatives for a dinner party at his house. G.K. Chettur was also present at that party. We had a good time and a good meal. The next day I sailed for India.

The hearty approval and enthusiastic appreciation of the various activities of the Indian independence movement and the Indian National Army in India was sufficient to dispel all our fears and most of our doubts. We, the Indians in East Asia always looked towards the Indian National Congress for inspiration and example. Our leaders, Rash Behari Bose and Netaji Subhas Chandra Bose, who organised and guided our movement repeatedly and earnestly appealed to the Indian National Congress and to Mahatma Gandhi in particular for help and guidance in all our endeavours for the liberation of our motherland. Mahatma Gandhi, the father of our nation, Jawaharlal Nehru, the undisputed leader of India and all other leaders of India were at that time in prison and the British government in India did not allow even a chance suggestion of approval or encouragement of our efforts reach us till the surrender of the INA, and so we had our fears as to whether our actions would receive approval in India.

My Days After Netaji

"Memory is the joy and sorrow of mankind."

Was there ever a freedom fighter so eminent, so daring, and so great as Netaji Subhas Chandra Bose? For more than a quarter of a century, millions of Indians were anxiously waiting to learn the truth about the disappearance of Netaji whom they regard as the foremost among the great freedom fighters of India. He was truly the greatest of our soldiers; the supreme commander of the Indian National Army, which fought a major war against the Anglo-American forces of occupation of India and won victories. Netaji's past clearly reveals that all his life he cared precious little for himself or like any other ordinary leader put self above nation in the matter of interests.

The Japanese wanted us to believe that Netaji had been involved in a plane crash on the island of Foremosa on 18 August 1945 and died subsequently of burns he had received. In fact, the Japanese published this story to save and protect Netaji from the Anglo-Americans. The Japanese military leaders and their government wanted to save him and protest him from any harm.

In 1956, the Government of India appointed an enquiry commission under Gen Shah Nawas Khan to enquire into the whereabouts of Netaji who had been missing. The commission, in the course of its work, visited Tokyo. The Japanese gave all sorts of facilities for the enquiry commission to enquire and endorse their story of the plane crash. General Shah Nawas Khan or anyone else in that position would not have done better under the circumstances. Most people in India never took that report seriously.

The "Forget-Netaji" attitude of many of our leaders, as also the Government of India, only prolonged the suspense and consequent agony of the admirers of Netaji. Prominent members of the Forward Bloc, members of Netaji's family, and some members of Parliament were able to rouse the Government of India to appoint a commission to enquire into the Netaji mystery, fourteen long years after the Shah Nawas Commission submitted its report.

Ever since the news of the Japanese plane crash involving Netaji, I had tried my best to find out the whereabouts of Netaji. My efforts along this line, mostly by letters to my friends in Japan, and some others in the Southeastern states were of no use and I could learn nothing of value regarding the missing leader. It is no wonder that I failed. The various rumours and stories often published in the news papers concerning Netaji were all untrue and the result of wishful thinking. I never paid heed to any such news.

The news item given by the well known journalist Jog, in June 1970, published in the 'Sunday Standard,' about the last moments of Netaji struck me as something important. Working on that news, I was soon able to go into the truth of the matter. The man who told Jog that he knew of the last moments of Netaji asserted that if he were to give out the news, that news would shock the capitals of the world. And he refused to reveal the secret to Jog. But I managed to share this secret with a common friend. He revealed his secret to a good friend of mine who approached him for the news at my instance. They being intimate friends, there was no difficulty in getting the news. But only a short account devoid of details could be obtained. He informed my friend that Netaji was shot dead by the Japanese. I could not get further information as to who shot Netaji and where and when the shooting took place. Certainly, those that perpetrated the cruel deed will never reveal their guarded secret. Shocked and grieved, I did not dare to speak about it even to my good friends for some time. The Japanese trapped and caged the lion, then shot him dead conveniently.

I did not know at first what to do with this truly heartrending news. After a few days of silence, I decided to write to the Japanese ambassador in New Delhi, giving specific details of the shocking deed. And, on 21 October 1970, the 27th anniversary day of the declaration the Provisional Government of Azad Hind by Netaji, I wrote requesting help to clear the mystery of Netaji's disappearance and to enable the Government of India to order the winding up of the Khosla Commission enquiring into the mystery. I charged the Japanese with the cruel murder of Netaji. I got a reply in turn which was typical of the Japanese. Those who know the Japanese mind know that whenever the Japanese have difficulty in revealing the truth, they will not hesitate to conceal the truth. The Japanese ambassador was no exception to this familiar Japanese trait. He did not care to deny or accept the charge of shooting Netaji to death. I am giving below the copy of the reply I received.

No.25/1434/790

Embassy of Japan,

New Delhi.

Dated: Oct. 28th, 1970.

Dear Pillai,

Our Embassy received your letter addressed to our ambassador dated October 21, 1970.

About the unfortunate death of Netaji Subhash Chandra Bose, our Embassy is aware of the report of the three-member committee (headed by Gen Shah Nawas Khan) of 1956 and also the present enquiry of the Khosla Commission. Our Embassy is not in a position to make any further comment on your letter.

Sincerely yours,

Sd/-

K. Uchida,

Second secretary.

We know of the Khosla Commission (1970) appointed by the Government of India to enquire into the disappearance of Netaji Subhash Chandra Bose. Whatever might be the expectation, I had no faith in the success of the mission. Let us not forget that Gen Shah Nawas Khan with two very competent members of the INA to assist him in the very same mission (1956), failed to find out the truth of the whereabouts of Netaji. Are there many among us who are prepared to believe that Justice Khosla will succeed where Gen Shah Nawas Khan failed fourteen years ago? He is very late and it is no fault of his. He was appointed by the Government of India to prepare his report after enquiry. The report surely will conclude that Netaji is dead but will again agree with the Japanese story of the plane crash. Any further enquiry as well as the present one will only be a waste of Indian tax payers' money. The Japanese government was not so far approached at the governmental level, to inquire into the mystery around the death of Netaji. The false alarm of the plane crash was repeated so many times, and so the Japanese need not tell the truth any more. Netaji is dead.

I then wrote to the home minister, Government of India, informing him the cause of the death of Netaji, and also enclosing copies of my letter to the Japanese ambassador and the reply received. I did not get a reply and so I wrote to the Khosla Commission in New Delhi giving a full account of the details of the news, my efforts to inform the authorities, and my inability to appear before the commission to submit my report personally. I enclosed copies of my letters to the home minister, the Japanese ambassador, and also the reply from the concerned embassy. The reply from the Khosla commission is given below.

K.R. Ramaswamy,
Asst. Secretary,

DOP Nop.\4/14/70... NIC

Government of India,

Neaji Enquiry Commission,

Second Floor,

Reserve Bank Building,

Parliament Street,

New Delhi.

12th November 1970.

Dear Shri Pillai,

Please refer to your letter of the 5th November 1970 offering your assistance in the matter of the enquiry entrusted to this commission. We welcome your kind assistance and hope to make use of the same in due course.

Will it be possible for you to send me a little more detail about the information regarding Netaji which is reported to have been communicated by the Indian businessman about Netaji?

With regards,

Yours sincerely

Sd/-

K. Ramaswamy.

My efforts for any further information regarding the last moments of Netaji were unrewarded and so I informed Mr. Ramaswamy of the Khosla Commission of my inability to comply with his request. Sometime later, I read in the papers about the Khosla Commission's sittings at Trivandrum where K.P. Kesava Menon, one who never had seen Netaji while in Singapore, as he was in Japanese prison till the end of the war, and M. Sivaram, who had been away in Tokyo, from where he escaped to South Siam, just before the Japanese surrender in August 1945, gave evidence. The commission did not care to inform me of its visit to Trivandrum. I do not wish to make any comments on the working of the Khosla Commission but I have to call a spade a spade. Like many others, I too, awaited the report of the Khosla Commission on Netaji's death. It remains to be seen whether the Japanese government will ever give out the truth about Netaji. There is no need for them as they can always hold out the story of the plane crash. Isn't it now over 75 years since Netaji was reported missing? The mystery around the disappearance of Netaji is now reduced to his death either by the conventional plane crash story or by untold cold-blooded murder. In either case, Netaji is dead. Even if the Japanese care to admit the shooting, what are we going to do about it? We can at the most give them credit for admission of this important truth, while nurturing in our hearts a deep sense of hatred for them at the same time for cruelly assassinating our beloved Netaji and even motivating us to retaliate in return for the costly loss. But, is it possible and more so necessary, the anguished minds ask us again, weighing the pros and cons of the contemplated action in question.

Since Netaji is dead, the ashes which the Japanese are keeping in a certain shrine in Tokyo, are his ashes. The letter I wrote to the prime minister, requesting to take necessary steps to bring the sacred ashes to India, on the occasion of the freedom celebrations in India, has been duly acknowledged. The reply I got is given below:

S.K. Upal,   Ministry of External Affairs

Under Secretary (J)   New Delhi – 11

15th March 1972.

Dear Shri Pillai,

Please refer to your letter dated 29th February 1972, addressed to the prime minister, pertaining to Netaji Bose's ashes, now being kept in a shrine in Tokyo. Your letter has been sent to the ministry of home affairs who are dealing with this subject and constituted an enquiry commission concerning Netajl's death under Justice Khosla recently.

Yours sincerely,

Sd/-

S.K. Upal.

Netaji Subhas Candra Bose's charming personality, dynamic leadership, and the endearing generalship will ever be remembered by India with deep sense of gratitude. History will record his slogan 'Chalo Delhi' and his greeting 'Jai Hind' as befitting his greatness. Like Mahatma Gandhi, father of the nation, who died a martyr at the hands of an assassin, Godse, Netaji too had to die, we believe, by the guns of an unknown Japanese.

"I have unearthed the truth, I must say, regarding the disappearance of our beloved leader Netaji, which was indeed baffling Indians well nigh for more than half a century. It is based on the words of an individual, who is of Indian origin, and a man of repute in Japan. He was very closely associated with our freedom movement and he took a prominent part in its early stages. Until otherwise proved, I think we have to accept that Netaji was shot dead by the Japanese. Let us, therefore, conclude that Netaji is was alive even after, as some people want us to believe."

"I am not in a position to find fault with the actions of the government or the leaders of our great country for not doing what was proper at the proper time and for not finding out the truth of a matter of great national importance to India. I am sure the Japanese did not very much care whether the shooting to death of their former ally and great friend amounted to an unjust and cruel murder. Surely they lack the moral strength and courage to admit this truth. And they have a great advantage that they propagated a false alarm, to the effect that Netaji's death was due to burns in the plane crash. No one then in India questioned the Japanese or demanded a satisfactory explanation from the Japanese government. Whose fault was that? Are we not good friends of the British even now, in spite of their past exploitation of Indians for more than a century? They have shot many eminent sons and daughters of India. So, naturally, there is not going to be any retaliation against the Japanese, too, for what they have done to Netaji."

"Is anybody really guilty of gross indifference and disrespectful attitude towards the Netaji episode? If so, who are they? These are the questions which deserve to be considered and answers obtained! And if it is pointed out that there is no ground for such questions, I am ever prepared to withdraw them in this regard."

"In any other democratic country, it would never have been possible to beguile a people to this extent as is clearly shown by the appointment of the Khosla Commission to enquire into the Netaji mystery. He disappeared on 18 August 1945. Some eleven years after the disappearance of Netaji, Gen Shah Nawas Khan, who was one of the trusted followers of Netaji, visited Japan and enquired about Netaji and we have the report of that enquiry. Now, 17 years after, the Khosla Commission was constituted for the very same purpose. What a farce? And who are paying for the expenses of these commissions, but the poor people of India who really foot the bill for these commissions' slow, costly proceedings."

"There were great national tragedies in other countries over which the people of those countries grieved. We too are no exception. We had our colossal tragedies. Let us face them boldly, learn what we ought to learn from them and go forward with determination to work for our nation's future. There is not much use in crying over the death of Netaji or Mahatma Gandhi. The loss of Netaji is no doubt a great national misfortune. Let us remember him with due gratitude for all his great efforts for the furtherance of our struggle for freedom. We achieved our freedom but he did not live to see our country free. When he died, his last words truly might have been "Jai Hind."

There may be differences of opinion on the views I have expressed. But anyone can easily understand that I have expressed only the obvious. I have not mentioned names of persons involved for reasons my own. Had anyone wanted any information in this regard, l would have willingly supplied the same. The government authorities in India are as much to be blamed for not getting the truth of Netaji's last moments as is the government of Japan for not giving us the truth which they could have given as a friendly gesture.

Nothing much will be gained by finding fault with the two governments. Netaji is no more. He died long ago. We have to accept this fact and put up with it. As Indians we would like to learn all about his death, only if the Japanese are pleased to co-operate with us. Let us try our best to emulate his greatness by words and deeds. Let us draw inspiration from memories of this great man whom we all regard the crowning soldier of Indian freedom.

Long live Netaji,

JAI HIND

www.ingramcontent.com/pod-product-compliance
Lightning Source LLC
Chambersburg PA
CBHW031228250726
48655CB00005B/1851